SUPERMAN ACTION COMICS
THE OZ EFFECT

SUPERMAN ACTION COMICS
THE OZ EFFECT

DAN JURGENS
ROB WILLIAMS
writers

VIKTOR BOGDANOVIC
DAN JURGENS * RYAN SOOK * GUILLEM MARCH * WILL CONRAD
JONATHAN GLAPION * JAY LEISTEN * TREVOR SCOTT * SCOTT HANNA
artists

MIKE SPICER
HI-FI
colorists

ROB LEIGH
letterer

NICK BRADSHAW and **BRAD ANDERSON**
collection cover artists

MIKE COTTON PAUL KAMINSKI Editors - Original Series * **ANDREA SHEA** Assistant Editor - Original Series
JEB WOODARD Group Editor - Collected Editions * **ROBIN WILDMAN** Editor - Collected Edition
STEVE COOK Design Director - Books * **DAMIAN RYLAND** Publication Design

BOB HARRAS Senior VP - Editor-in-Chief, DC Comics
PAT McCALLUM Executive Editor, DC Comics

DAN DiDIO Publisher * **JIM LEE** Publisher & Chief Creative Officer
BOBBIE CHASE VP - New Publishing Initiatives & Talent Development * **DON FALLETTI** VP - Manufacturing Operations & Workflow Management
LAWRENCE GANEM VP - Talent Services * **ALISON GILL** Senior VP - Manufacturing & Operations * **HANK KANALZ** Senior VP - Publishing Strategy & Support Services
DAN MIRON VP - Publishing Operations * **NICK J. NAPOLITANO** VP - Manufacturing Administration & Design
NANCY SPEARS VP - Sales * **MICHELE R. WELLS** VP & Executive Editor, Young Reader

SUPERMAN: ACTION COMICS: THE OZ EFFECT

DC Comics, 2900 West Alameda Ave., Burbank, CA 91505. Printed by LSC Communications, Kendallville, IN, USA. 5/10/19. First Printing.
ISBN: 978-1-4012-8786-3

Library of Congress Cataloging-in-Publication Data is available.

Only Human
PART 1
IT IS SO EASY TO RESENT HIM.
HUMAN BEINGS ARE COMPLEX AND CONFUSED, THEY ARE A CHURNING MASS OF DESIRES AND FEARS AT ANY GIVEN MOMENT. A WHITE NOISE OF BEMUSEMENT.
WE ARE NOT BINARY. GOOD AND EVIL WOULD BE BLISSFUL DEFINITIONS. UNATTAINABLE CERTAINTY. FOREVER OUT OF REACH.
HE, HOWEVER, IS GOOD.
IT IS SO EASY TO RESENT HIM...
ROB WILLIAMS Writer
GUILLEM MARCH Artist
HI-FI Color
ROB LEIGH Letters
GUILLEM MARCH Cover
NEIL EDWARDS AND JEROMY COX Variant Cover
PAUL KAMINSKI Associate Editor
MIKE COTTON Editor
EDDIE BERGANZA Group Editor
SUPERMAN created by Jerry Siegel and Joe Shuster.
SUPERBOY created by Jerry Siegel.
By special arrangement with the Jerry Siegel family.

CLARK...
CAN YOU HEAR ME?
I CAN HEAR YOU, LOIS. THE EARPIECE WORKS GREAT.
WHAT'S WRONG?

YOU'RE NOT HERE! THAT'S WHAT'S WRONG!
YOUR SON SAYS HELLO.
SAY HEY TO DAD FOR ME!
HEY, JON!
I DID THE PACKING. I JUST... NEEDED TO GET OUT FOR A WHILE.
I'M WORRIED ABOUT YOU. YOU'VE BEEN THROUGH A LOT LATELY. GODSLAYER, THE REVENGE SQUAD, MXYZPT--
PLEASE DON'T SAY THAT NAME.
AND NOW THE MOVE TO METROPOLIS. LEAVING HAMILTO COUNTY. YOU NEED A BREAK.
WE NEED A BREAK. OUR LITTLE TRIP WASN'T ENOUGH.
NO... YOU'RE RIGHT, WE HAVE BEEN THROUGH A LOT LATELY...

...AND WE'VE COME THROUGH.
I FEEL *GOOD,* LOIS.
I FEEL...
...OPTIMISTIC.
Hmm. WE'VE TALKED ABOUT TEMPTING FATE, BIG BLUE.
I HAVE TO GO. I'M PICKING UP SOMETHING A FEW HUNDRED MILES FROM HERE...
...GUNFIRE. SCREAMS.
SO MUCH FOR OPTIMISM.
NO. THE PEOPLE CAN BE OPTIMISTIC.
HELP'S COMING.

CAUCASUS MOUNTAINS, GEORGIA.
KRAKKAKAKA
AH!
‹RUN! RUN! THEY'RE KILLING US!›*
*TRANSLATED FROM GEORGIAN. --Cotton
‹WOLVES...›
‹EVEN THE ANIMALS HAVE JOINED THEM!›
‹AHHH!›
THWAKKK
SIT!

‹...MY GOD...›
THE WOLF. SOMETHING IN ITS NECK...
...SOME KIND OF COMPUTER CHIP.
I'VE SEEN THESE BEFORE.
THEY'RE MIND TICKS.
THE ANIMALS. SOME OF THESE GUNMEN, THEY'RE BEING CONTROLLED.
I KNOW WHO'S BEHIND THIS.
KRAKKAKADAKA
STOP...
...THAT!
FZZZSHHH

MACHINIST!
SHOW YOURSELF!
HELLO, SUPERMAN.
YOU'RE A LONG WAY FROM HOME.

SAVE IT FOR THE PRISON CELL!
KRUNCH
OH, COME NOW...
YOU CAN'T REALLY BE THIS NAIVE...
YANK
YOU KNOW I'M NOT *REALLY* HERE. THIS IS JUST ANOTHER NOBODY I'VE TAKEN TO DO MY HANDIWORK.
I DIDN'T START THIS CIVIL WAR. BUT I'M HAPPY TO PROVIDE THE TECH AND THE WEAPONS TO GIVE IT MORE *SCALE...*
...IF SOMEONE PAYS ME ENOUGH.
HOW DO YOU FIND THE *REAL* MACHINIST, SUPERMAN?
WHEN I CAN POSSESS ANYONE OR ANYTHING TO DO *MY* WORK FOR ME?
BESIDES, ALL I'M DOING IS GIVING PEOPLE WHAT THEY *WANT!*
YOU DO KNOW THAT, RIGHT?
HUMANITY DOESN'T NEED ANY ENCOURAGEMENT TO DO THIS. JUST TURN ON THE NEWS AT ANY GIVEN--

--UCK!
Ah, THERE IT IS.
THIS IS THE MASTER CHIP FOR THE AREA. I CAN HEAR THE SIGNAL IT'S SENDING OUT.
KZZZT
DESTROY THIS...
"...AND IT'S LIKE HITTING THE OFF SWITCH.
"THEY'LL WAKE UP WITH A HORRIBLE HEADACHE. WHICH IS PROBABLY THE LEAST OF WHAT THEY DESERVE..."
...BUT THE REAL MACHINIST IS STILL OUT THERE...
Hmmm...
WHERE HAVE I SEEN THIS CIRCUITRY BEFORE?
<SUPERMAN! COME! YOU HAVE TO SEE THIS!>
OH, HI. THERE'S NO NEED TO...
<MORE ATTACKS! THE SAME ATTACKS! ACROSS THE WORLD!>

YOU WANT ME TO LOOK AT THE TV?
WHY DO YOU WANT ME TO...
...OH.
IS THAT... IS THAT IN GERMANY?
THE SAME THING IS HAPPENING THERE...
(SAME ATTACKS IN DIFFERENT COUNTRIES!)
I'VE SEEN THIS CIRCUITRY BEFORE. IF I USE MY MICROSCOPIC VISION...
MAYBE I CAN...
...I...
LEX.

LUTHOR!
NOW NOW.
WE DON'T DO THAT ANYMORE, REMEMBER?

"AND, LO, HE FLOATS THERE.
"SILENTLY JUDGING THE HUMAN--"
I BELIEVED IN YOU.
THKKK
WHERE DID YOU GET THIS?

I PULLED IT FROM THE NECK OF A TERRORIST ATTACKING A VILLAGE IN GEORGIA NEAR THE RUSSIAN BORDER. THE CIVIL WAR THERE--
THIS... IT'S SOME KIND OF CEREBRAL CORTEX GRAFT. POWER JABS UP AND ALONG THE LONGITUDINAL FISSURE ENSURING COMPLIANCE...
LUTHOR...
THEY'VE... BASTARDIZED MY SEMICONDUCTOR DESIGN.
IT'S A MIND CONTROL CHIP, LUTHOR.
THEY'VE STOLEN MY WORK!
THIS IS LEXCORP MATERIAL.
THE MACHINIST IS POSSESSING PEOPLE AND ANIMALS WITH IT. WHATEVER CAN KILL MORE.
CREATE MORE *TERROR.*
HE'S USING IT TO HELP DESTABILIZE THE REGION. INTENSIFY THE EXISTING CONFLICT.
YOUR DESIGN. *YOUR* LOGO IS ON IT.
REALLY? I AM THE VICTIM HERE! THE AGGRIEVED PARTY. SOMEONE HAS STOLEN *MY* WORK.
BUT YOU THINK I'M BEHIND THIS?

YOU ARE SUPERMAN. YOU STAND FOR--
YOU KNOW WHAT I STAND FOR.
TRUTH. YOU STAND FOR TRUTH. SO HEAR IT.
I *DIDN'T* DO THIS.
AND THERE'S A VERY GOOD REASON YOU SHOULD BELIEVE THAT.
AND THAT WOULD BE?
BECAUSE IF I *WERE* RESPONSIBLE, THIS PLAN WOULD HAVE *SUCCEEDED.*
Hrm...IF YOU ARE TELLING THE TRUTH AND YOU REALLY DIDN'T DO THIS...
...YOU CAN HELP ME STOP IT.
YES...
THE WORLD'S GREATEST SUPERHERO IS ON THE CASE!
ME.

Heh.
A TEAM-UP THEN...
LATER.
THE LEXCORP SUPERCONDUCTORS IN THE MIND TICKS EMIT A UNIQUE ENERGY SIGNATURE. AN ENERGY SIGNATURE THAT ONLY I KNOW ABOUT.
AND ONE I CAN TRACK BACK TO THEIR SOURCE.
WE'RE COMING UP ON THE KASHMIR/INDIA BORDER.

LUTHOR... WHY WOULD YOU NEED TO BE ABLE TO TRACK--
MASS CONFLAGRATION OF SIGNALS BELOW. THIS MUST BE IT.
YES.
I'D SAY THIS IS PROBABLY IT.
MISSILES! MOVE!
THOOOM
AH!
LUTHOR!
THOOOOOOOM

...LUTHOR?
I'VE GOT Y--
AH!
THUNKK

AH YES...
...WELCOME TO INDIA.
HE'S MILITARIZED ELEPHANTS AND TIGERS?
KRAKKAKKA
NOT SOMETHING YOU SEE EVERY DAY...

KRAKAKAKAKAKA
IT SEEMS ANIMALS HATE YOU.
THEY'RE POSSESSED BY MIND TICKS!
OR ANIMALS HATE YOU-- ELEPHANTS!
OOOFFFFF!
TAKE CARE OF THE GUNMEN!
NON-LETHAL WEAPONS ONLY, LUTHOR.
AH, IF YOU ONLY KNEW WHAT THIS SUIT WAS CAPABLE OF...
BOOOOM
THE MAIN SIGNAL FOR THE LEXCORP CHIPS IS NEAR HERE. AND MISSILES. THEN THIS WELCOMING COMMITTEE...
"I'D SAY YOU MAY BE ABOUT TO MEET THE REAL MACHINIST, SUPERMAN."
...THEY FOUND ME...
GOOD.
NOW THEY CAN SERVE ME.
THKKK

ZZZZZZZ
NANO-DRONES! LOOK OUT!
MY FORCE FIELD WILL...
AH!
THNKK
CONTACT ACHIEVED, MR. LUTHOR. THIS IS AN ENHANCED CHIP. REMOVE THIS, YOU FRY THE CEREBRAL CORTEX OF THE SUBJECT. SO, NO EASY OUTS HERE.
NOW...
KILL SUPERMAN.
LEX.
I NEED YOU TO FIGHT THIS...
...WE CAN TAKE THEM DOWN TOGETHER.
"ALWAYS JUDGING ME..."
I'M SORRY, SUPERMAN...

...I JUST CAN'T CONTROL MYSELF.
"IT IS SO EASY TO RESENT HIM.
"I WONDER IF IT'S HARDER TO KILL HIM."

Only Human PART 2
THE TRUTH
BOOOOM
I AM TRYING TO FIGHT THIS, SUPERMAN.
REALLY, I AM.
BUT I'M ONLY HUMAN.
ROB WILLIAMS Writer
GUILLEM MARCH Artist
HI-FI Color
ROB LEIGH Letters
GUILLEM MARCH & TOMEU MOREY Cover
NEIL EDWARDS & JEROMY COX Variant Cover
PAUL KAMINSKI and MIKE COTTON Editors
EDDIE BERGANZA Group Editor
SUPERMAN created by Jerry Siegel and Joe Shuster. By special arrangement with the Jerry Siegel family.

MOTHER...
...BOX TECH...
USING THIS SUIT IS A DELICATE BALANCE...
...ONE RISKS LOSING ONESELF...
KRUNNNCHH
IT'S INTERESTING.
MY MIND-TICKS OFTEN ACTIVATE THE SUBJECT'S SUBCONSCIOUS IN A WAY I DID NOT EXPECT.
I'M JUST GIVING PEOPLE WHAT THEY SECRETLY ALWAYS WANTED. I SUPPOSE...
"...YOU CAN THINK OF THIS AS A KIND OF THERAPY."
KZZZ

FZZZSSH
THE MORE YOU USE THE APOKOLIPTIAN TECH...
...THE MORE LIKE DARKSEID YOU BECOME.
AH!!
EVERYTHING THAT'S HAPPENED LATELY. EVERYTHING THE WORLD KEEPS SENDING AT ME.
BOOM
FFSSHOOOM
BUT YOU, THE WAY YOU *CHANGED*...
...YOU INSPIRED ME, LEX.
SUPERMAN, I...I CAN'T...
YOU'D REINFORCED MY HOPE...
...FOR EVEN THE WORST OF HUMANITY.
THOOM

HE PROBABLY THINKS THE MIND-TICK'S CONTROL IS DISTANCE RELATED.
IT'S NOT.

LET'S BE READY FOR THEM WHEN THEY RETURN.
PRIME ALL WEAPONS.
THINK, LEX.
YOU'RE THE SMARTEST MAN ON THE PLANET. YOUR CIRCUITRY'S IN THAT MIND-TICK. YOU MUST BE ABLE TO COME UP WITH A WAY TO BREAK THIS.

THE MIND-TICK CAN'T HAVE BEEN BUILT TO DEAL WITH APOKOLIPTIAN PHYSIOLOGY. AND THE MORE YOU USE THE APOKOLIPTIAN TECHNOLOGY...
YOUR WORDS...
YOU CAN FIGHT THIS.

...JUST WORDS.
DON'T YOU GET IT?
YOU ARE NOT HUMAN.
YOU WILL NEVER BE HUMAN.
YOU'LL NEVER KNOW WHAT IT'S LIKE. TO FEEL...OUT OF CONTROL.
YOU WANT US TO BE...GODS. TO LIVE UP TO YOUR STANDARDS. WELL, CONGRATULATIONS!
NOW I AM THE GOD HERE!!
NOW YOU CAN KNOW HOW IT FEELS TO BE INFERIOR.

WHAT ARE YOU... ?
BOOM
BOOM
BOOM
I KNEW YOU'D STOP MOST OF THEM BEFORE THEY GOT TO YOU BUT...
...YOU'RE NOT INFALLIBLE.
KRYPTONITE DARTS. I HAVE HAD THEM IN THE SUIT FOR SOME TIME NOW.
JUST IN CASE.
I HAVE LONG BELIEVED...
...ONLY A HUMAN CAN TRULY PROTECT HUMANITY.

BUT...
...BEING HERE NOW?
...THIS ISN'T HUMAN, IS IT?
POWER...
BOOOOM
SUPERMAN!!!
THAT'S RIGHT, LITTLE TOY.
KILL HIM.

I...
YES.
ACTIVATING ALL SUIT WEAPONRY! ALL MOTHER BOX ENERGIES!
ACTIVATE EVERYTHING I CREATED!
BOOM
BOOOM
ACTIVATE EVERYTHING!!!
AAAAHHH!!!
FZZZFSSSH
BOOOOOM
HA.
HE'S HITTING HIM WITH EVERYTHING HE'S GOT!

GGGAAAHH!!!
FZZZSSHHH
AH!
FSSSHHBBZZZ...
I...
...AM...
...COUNTING ON...
FLICH
...YOU.

IMPOSSIBLE.
NO. NOT IMPOSSIBLE AT ALL, MACHINIST.
YOU FORGET WHO YOU'RE DEALING WITH.

HOW?
HOW?
THERE IS NO WAY TO BREAK THE CONTROL OF THE MASTER CHIPS!
KZZT
POWER, RIGHT?
KZZT
KZZT
KZZT
THAT'S WHY YOU WERE FIRING ALL THE APOKOLIPTIAN TECH AT ME? YOU WERE DELIBERATELY TRYING TO OVERLOAD THE SUIT.
KZZT
THE MIND-TICK WAS BUILT FOR HUMAN PHYSIOLOGY, NOT APOKOLIPS TECH.
Uh... YES...
THAT'S EXACTLY WHY I FIRED EVERYTHING AT YOU... erm.
MY SUIT'S RIED. ALL WEAPONS AND DEFENSE SYSTEMS DOWN. I'M OUT.
THEY'RE COMING!
IT'S OKAY.
NOW IT'S MY TURN.

BOOM
KROOM
NO. I DON'T THINK SO...
NO RUNNING FROM THIS.

YOU'VE BEEN ACCELERATING CIVIL WARS FOR MONEY.
AND I WANT TO KNOW WHO WAS PAYING YOU.
WHOSE ORDERS YOU WERE FOLLOWING.
WHO WANTED YOU TO BUILD THESE ROBOTS?
SMASSHHH
ANSWER ME.
WHICH ONE OF YOU IS THE MACHINIST?
WE...
...WE SURRENDER...
ALL OF US.
HE--THE MACHINIST--HE RAN AWAY.

GOT YOU.
I DON'T KNOW WHAT YOU'RE TALKING ABOUT! I WAS JUST TAKING ORDERS! HIS ORDERS!
IT'S NOT ME, I SWEAR!

HE HAS X-RAY VISION, YOU FOOL.
HE CAN PICK UP ALL SORTS OF ELECTROMAGNETIC FIELDS WITH THAT. INCLUDING THE ENERGY SIGNATURES OF YOUR MIND-TICKS.

I'VE PIERCED YOUR DISGUISES BEFORE, MACHINIST. I KNOW WHAT YOU'RE HIDING UNDERNEATH.
...
SO YOU KNOW MY TRUE FACES...
*SEE SUPERMAN: THE MEN OF TOMORROW. --P & C

SORRY.
GUESS I SEE THROUGH PEOPLE.

I LOVE A HAPPY ENDING.
THE CIVIL WARS WERE GOING ON BEFORE THE MACHINIST GOT INVOLVED. PEOPLE WERE DYING. HE JUST...PUSHED IT FURTHER, IS ALL.
THAT, I'M AFRAID, IS HUMAN NATURE.
NOTHING YOU CAN DO ABOUT IT.
...MAYBE.
...THANK YOU.
FOR WHAT?
THE MIND-TICK... YOU CAME UP WITH A SOLUTION. OVERLOAD THE SUIT'S POWER BASELINES. AND, MOST IMPORTANTLY, YOU REMINDED ME OF SOMETHING CRUCIAL.
I AM THE *SMARTEST MAN IN THE WORLD.*
WHY DID THE MACHINIST STEAL YOUR CIRCUITRY, LEX? HOW WAS HE ABLE TO DO THAT?
I DON'T KNOW, BUT I WILL FIND OUT.
...
YOU'RE WELCOME.

METROPOLIS.
LATER.
Hmmm. CURIOUS.
SUIT CAMERA FOOTAGE, REWIND FOUR SECONDS AND FOCUS IN ON GRID 24B.
I'M SURE I SAW SOMETHING...
STOP! BLOW UP THAT GRID, PLEASE!
WHAT IS THAT? IT'S GLOWING...
IT'S NOT ONE OF THE MIND-TICKS.
SAVE THIS IMAGE TO MY PERSONAL DATABASE AND SEARCH FOR ALL INTERNET SIMILARITIES. INCLUDE THE DARK WEB IN THE SEARCH.
IT LOOKS LIKE A...
...TATTOO?
ALERT! INTRUDER! INTRUDER!
WHO...?

IMAGE.
DELETE ALL COPIES OF THAT IMAGE.
DELETED.
WHAT?
YOU WANT TO KNOW HOW I STOLE YOUR DESIGNS? YOUR INSIDIOUS CIRCUITRY?
BECAUSE I AM SMARTER THAN YOU.
YOU BUILT A POWER SIGNATURE INTO EACH MICRO-PROCESSOR THAT YOU COULD TRACK. ONE THAT YOU COULD SECRETLY ACCESS AFTER YOU SOLD IT ACROSS THE WORLD. AND NO ONE BUT YOU WOULD EVER KNOW.
HOW CRIMINAL.
NO! THAT WAS NOT MY INTENTION. I NEVER IMPLEMENTED IT. AND THE PLAN WAS TO PROTECT EARTH!
AN AIRTIGHT SECURITY GRID ONLY I COULD ACCESS. A POSSIBLE WEAPON AGAINST ALIEN INVASION!
I DON'T KNOW WHO YOU ARE, HOW YOU GOT IN HERE, OR BY WHAT MEANS YOU GAINED THIS INFORMATION.
BUT YOU WILL REGRET THIS!

YOU PROVE YOURSELF A PETULANT CHILD WHO REQUIRES...
...DISCIPLINE.
FZZZSSHZZZZH
AAAAAAHH!
DO YOU WANT TO KNOW *THE TRUTH,* LEX?
I'M AFRAID YOU WON'T LIKE IT VERY MUCH.

YOU ARE *NOT* HIM.

YOU WILL *NEVER* BE SUPERMAN.

EVEN WHEN YOU TRY TO DO GOOD, YOU CANNOT ESCAPE THE BASE INIQUITY OF YOUR RACE.
THIS IS JUST WHO YOU ARE. NO MATTER HOW HARD YOU TRY. CRAWLING AMIDST THE DETRITUS.
ALL OF YOU.

YOU ARE ONLY HUMAN. YOU WILL ONLY EVER *BE* HUMAN.
AND SOON YOU WILL BE GONE.
AH...
AH...

AH...

MY GOD...

HOPE

OZ

R.G.U.S. WEAPONIZATION CENTER.
BJECT 2201.
ETALLO.
PLEASE...
...SO PAINFUL...
...I CAN'T TAKE IT ANYMORE!
PLEASE LET ME GO!

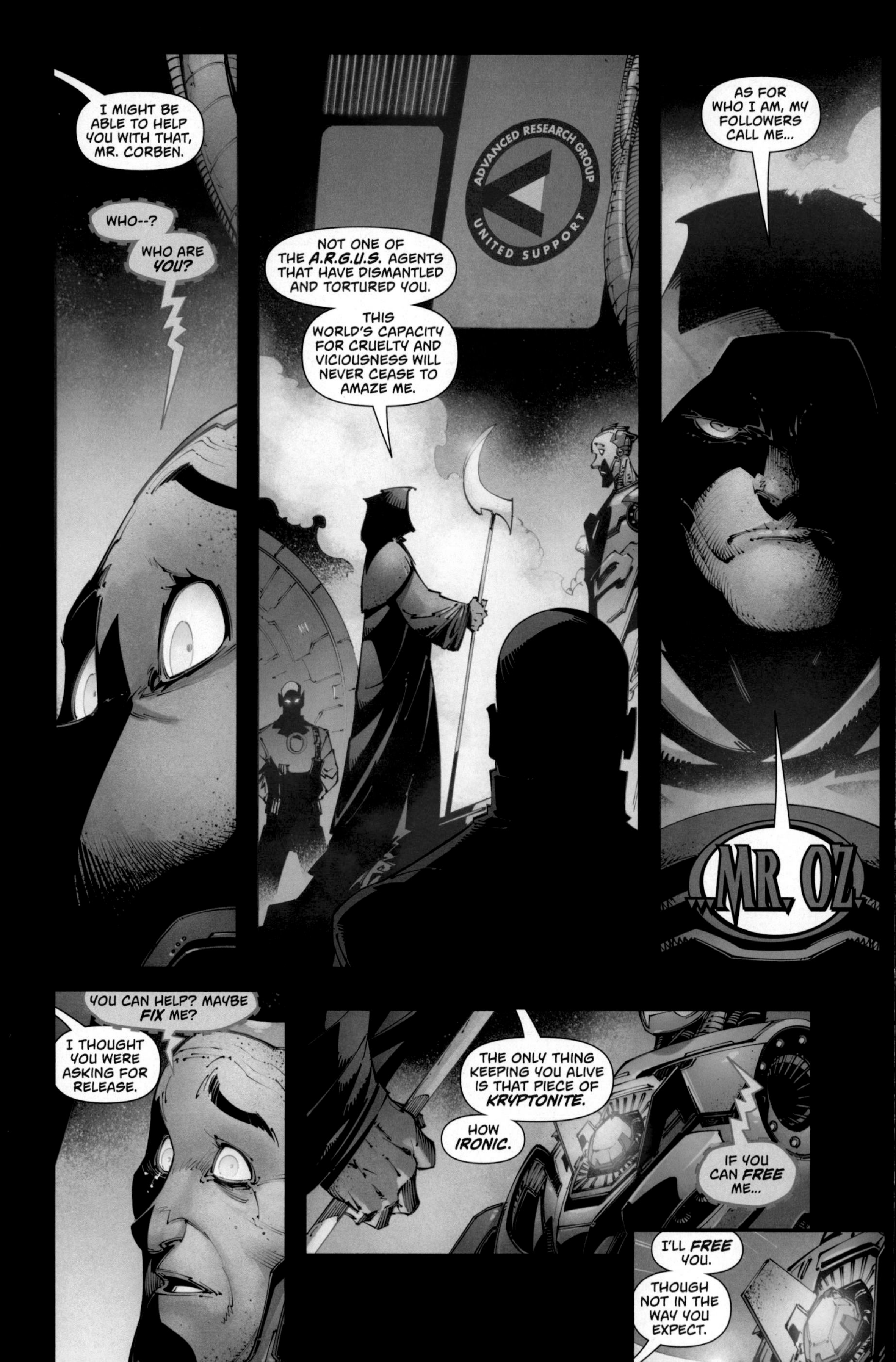
I MIGHT BE ABLE TO HELP YOU WITH THAT, MR. CORBEN.
WHO--?
WHO ARE YOU?
ADVANCED RESEARCH GROUP UNITED SUPPORT
NOT ONE OF THE A.R.G.U.S. AGENTS THAT HAVE DISMANTLED AND TORTURED YOU.
THIS WORLD'S CAPACITY FOR CRUELTY AND VICIOUSNESS WILL NEVER CEASE TO AMAZE ME.
AS FOR WHO I AM, MY FOLLOWERS CALL ME...
MR. OZ
YOU CAN HELP? MAYBE FIX ME?
I THOUGHT YOU WERE ASKING FOR RELEASE.
THE ONLY THING KEEPING YOU ALIVE IS THAT PIECE OF KRYPTONITE.
HOW IRONIC.
IF YOU CAN FREE ME...
I'LL FREE YOU.
THOUGH NOT IN THE WAY YOU EXPECT.

I'LL FREE YOU FROM YOUR WRETCHED LIFE.
NO! IF YOU DO THAT, I'LL--
...!
CHKKK
YOU WILL NEVER USE REMNANTS OF HIS WORLD AGAINST HIM AGAIN.
TAKE YOUR PLACES.
TOMORROW, WE BEGIN.
THAT'S WHEN HUMANITY WILL ULTIMATELY EXPOSE ITSELF...
FSASSH
...FOR THE SICK, TRAGIC, PERVERTED AND TWISTED ORGANISM IT IS.
AND YOU, KAL-EL...
...WILL COME TO REALIZE THAT THEY DON'T DESERVE YOU OR YOUR FAMILY.

METROPOLIS.
THIS IS ON YOU!
YEAH! SEE WHAT HAPPENS WHEN YOU ENGAGE IN A HIGH-SPEED CHASE?
IT'S YOUR FAULT THAT DELIVERY TRUCK ENDED UP IN THE RIVER!
IT'D BEEN HIJACKED.
GURGGGLE
SOMEONE WAS STEALING ITS CARGO!
SUMTHIN' VALUABLE? IN A GLOBAL HEALTH AGENCY TRUCK?
MEDICINE.
VACCINATIONS AGAINST A SMALLPOX VIRUS THAT'S RUNNING RAMPANT OVERSEAS.
IF WATER SEEPS IN THROUGH THE SEALS, IT'LL CONTAMINATE THE VACCINE.
MEANING THOUSANDS'LL DIE!
DIRECTOR SAWYER, TELL THEM!
I WAS ONLY DOING WHAT I HAD TO--!
SHAME!
ENOUGH.
I WAS HOPING YOU'D COME.

THE OZ EFFECT
PART ONE
WHOA!
LOOKIT!
IT'S HIM!
SUPERMAN!

DAN JURGENS WRITER
VIKTOR BOGDANOVIC PENCIL
JONATHAN GLAPION
JAY LEISTEN &
BOGDANOVIC INK
THE MEDICINE?
Global Health Agency
RUNNCH
WORKING ON IT, MAGGIE.
MADE IT IN TIME.
VIALS ARE STILL DRY.
MIKE SPICER COLOR
ROB LEIGH LETTERS
NICK BRADSHAW & BRAD ANDERSON COVER
NEIL EDWARDS & JEROMY COX VARIANT COVER
MIKE COTTON & PAUL KAMINSKI EDITORS
EDDIE BERGANZA GROUP EDITOR
I DON'T SEE A WEDDING RING! CAN I GIVE YOU MY NUMBER?
WAY TO GO, SUPERMAN!
NICE WORK, BLUE!
I'LL GET THIS WHERE IT NEEDS TO BE.
SUPERMAN created by JERRY SIEGEL and JOE SHUST
SUPERBOY created by JERRY SIEGEL.
BY SPECIAL ARRANGEMENT WITH THE JERRY SIEGEL FAMI

WHAT'RE YOU TRYING TO SAVE HIM FOR?
YEAH! HE WAS STEALING MEDICINE?!
LET HIM DIE ALREADY.
ARE YOU FOR REAL? IN METROPOLIS, WE TAKE CARE OF PEOPLE.
WISH EVERY PROBLEM WAS SO EASY TO SOLVE.
NO BAD GUYS TO PUNCH.
NO IMMINENT DISASTER TO NULLIFY.
AS SIMPLE AS FLYING A VACCINE OVERSEAS.
LOGAMBA IS DESTITUTE. WRACKED BY POLITICAL CONFLICT FOR YEARS.
NEITHER THE GOVERNMENT NOR REBELS SEEM TO CARE ABOUT LOGAMBANS ON THE WHOLE, SO IT'S UP TO THE REST OF THE WORLD TO STEP IN AND HELP.
MAKES ME APPRECIATE HOME.
IT MIGHT NOT BE PERFECT, BUT PEOPLE ARE HAPPY HERE.

ABLE TO ENJOY LIFE.
WITH HOPE FOR AN EVEN BETTER TOMORROW.
I HOPE YOU DON'T MIND JON COMING IN WITH ME FOR A BIT, PERRY.
WE'RE HAVING THE APARTMENT PAINTED AND THE FUMES ARE OVERWHELMING.
MIND?
WHY WOULD I MIND GETTING A CHANCE TO START SHAPING MY GODSON INTO A REPORTER?
WHOA, CHIEF.
"I'M THINKING LI'L CLARKY WOULD RATHER BE A PRO QUARTERBACK LIKE ME, RIGHT?
I'LL BET YOUR OLD MAN HAS TOLD YOU PLENTY ABOUT WHAT AN HONOR IT IS TO WORK WITH A STAR.
Uh-uh.
WHAT'S YOUR NAME AGAIN?

LOMBARD.
STEVE LOMBARD!
C'MON, KID. YOU MUSTA HEARD OF ME!
Um...

CHECK MY OFFICE AND YOU'LL SEE MY ROOKIE CARD AND SODER COLA GAME-OF-THE-WEEK MVP AWARD ON DISPLAY!
MAYBE ANOTHER TIME, MR. LOMBARD.
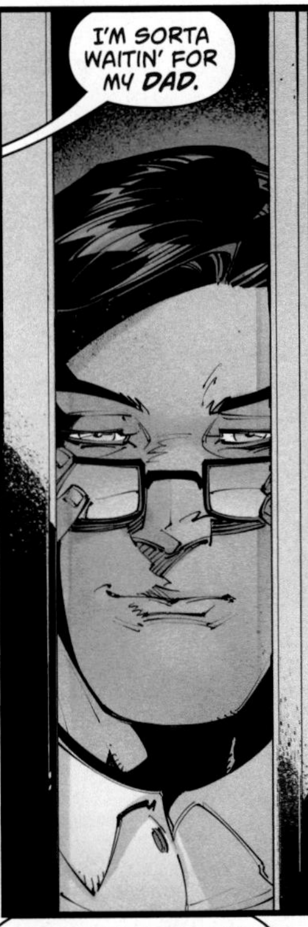
I'M SORTA WAITIN' FOR MY DAD.

TELL YOU WHAT, NEXT TIME YOU AND THE OLD MAN ARE FREE, I'LL GET US FIFTY-YARD-LINE SEATS TO A METEORS GAME.
THANKS FOR THE OFFER, STEVE.

I'LL CHECK THE CALENDAR AND GET BACK TO YOU.
CLARK, I CAN'T BEGIN TO TELL YOU HOW HAPPY I AM TO HAVE YOU KIDS LIVING BACK IN THE CITY AGAIN.
LIFE ISN'T THE SAME WITHOUT LOIS LANE AND CLARK KENT WORKING AT THE PLANET.
WAIT-- I GOT AN EVEN BETTER IDEA.

I'LL GET YOU AN OLD-SCHOOL, TOTALLY AUTHENTIC METEORS STEVE LOMBARD THROWBACK JERSEY!
MOST AWESOME THING A KID LIKE YOU COULD HOPE TO WEAR--GUARANTEED!
WHATTAYA SAY?
Uh...

IF HE ONLY KNEW...
...THAT JON HAS SOMETHING FAR BETTER TO WEAR?
AND ALREADY LEADS A LIFE...

"...THAT HAS GIVEN HIM A CHANCE TO EXPERIENCE THE INCREDIBLE?"
EARTH.
ITS PEOPLE ARE BRUTAL SAVAGES.
THEY TRICK THEMSELVES INTO THINKING THEY'RE BENEVOLENT...
...BUT IN THE END, ALL THEY CARE ABOUT IS THEMSELVES.
NOW, THE TIME HAS COME FOR THEM TO LOOK IN THE MIRROR...
"...AND SEE HOW MONSTROUS THEY TRULY ARE."
SORRY, FELLAS, BUT CORPORATE IS CUTTING BACK.
I'VE SPENT MY WHOLE LIFE WORKING HERE!
CALM SEAS, CAP'N. DRINK?
TWELVE-HOUR DAYS FOR PENNIES. YOU'RE CLEANIN' UP, BOSS.
THEY DON'T CALL IT A SWEATSHOP FOR NOTHING.
OH NO.
REBEL GUERRILLAS.
CAREFUL YOU DON'T HIT THE HORN.
IT'S THE ONLY REASON FOR KILLIN' THAT RHINO.
THEY LIVE ON THE EDGE OF CHAOS...
...IT'S TIME TO GIVE THEM A PUSH.
THEIR SUPERMAN CAN'T SAVE THEM FROM THEMSELVES.

WE GOT LAID OFF 'CUZ A' THEM, YOU KNOW.
THEY COME TO THIS COUNTRY AND WORK FOR HALF WHAT WE DO.
AIN'T EVEN CITIZENS.
YOU'RE RIGHT.
AN' IF SOMEONE DON'T TAKE A STAND, IT'LL KEEP HAPPENIN'.
DO YOU REALIZE WHAT THAT MEDICINE WOULD BE WORTH ON THE BLACK MARKET?
THINK OF THE GUNS WE COULD BUY!
SO LET'S TAKE IT.
LEXOIL TAKES US AWAY FROM OUR FAMILIES FOR MONTHS AT A TIME.
WE DESERVE A LITTLE FUN ON THE JOB.
DRINK UP!
STAGGOIL
INDEED.
NAMELESS BRATS WITH NO FUTURE. AS GOOD AS SLAVES.
WE CAN DO ANYTHING WE WANT.
I TAKE WHAT I WANT!
B-DAM
WHO CARES IF RHINOS ARE PROTECTED IN THE PRESERVE?
THEY HAVE NO RIGHT TO TELL US WHAT WE CAN HUNT.
TODAY, MAN PROVES HIS TRUE NATURE.
OPEN THE DOOR...
...AND THIS MISBEGOTTEN RACE WILL RUN RIGHT THROUGH, PROVING HOW UNDESERVING THEY REALLY ARE.

WE'RE OFF FOR SOME LUNCH.
IT'S BIBBO'S SUPER BURGER DAY AT THE ACE O' CLUBS!
AWESOME!
WHOA. HEY, CHIEF, MY PHONE IS BLOWIN' UP.

MINE, TOO, OLSEN.
I'VE NEVER SEEN SO MANY SIMULTANEOUS ALERTS COME THROUGH.

OIL TANKER RUPTURED ON SHORE... PRISON RIOT IN THE MIDWEST...WORKPLACE SHOOTINGS...

ALASKAN COAST
4 BREAKING NEWS
WAR BREAKING OUT IN LOGAMBA...
RACIAL DISPUTES, TERRORIST ACTS, WIDESPREAD VIOLENCE EVERYWHERE...
THIS IS MORE THAN ANYONE CAN HANDLE! EVEN...

SUPERMAN!

SO MANY THINGS COMING AT ONCE.
COINCIDENCE?
THOOM
OR SOMETHING MORE?
I GAVE EVERYTHING TO THIS COMPANY!
GOT INJURED SO MANY TIMES ON THE LINE--
--THAT I LITERALLY BLED FOR IT!
BUT I KEPT ON WORKIN' EVEN THOUGH IT WAS CRIPPLIN' ME!
THEN YOU PEOPLE CAME ALONG.
¡DETÉNGASE! ¡POR FAVOR!
YOU WORK CHEAP-- DON'T SPEAK ENGLISH SO YOU CAN'T TALK BACK OR EVEN ASK FOR A PENNY MORE...
YOU COST ME MY JOB!
MY LIVELIHOOD!
FOR THAT--
--YOU PAY!
BRAKKA BRAKK

STOP THIS.
¡GRACIAS A DIOS!
WHY?!
THEY STOLE FROM ME!
RUINED ME!
THE ONLY PERSON RESPONSIBLE FOR THE BLACKNESS SMOTHERING YOUR SOUL--
--IS YOU.
OFFICERS, MAKE SURE THESE PEOPLE ARE SAFE AND CARED FOR.
I HAVE TO GO.
ANYTHING YOU SAY, SUPERMAN!

HATED TO LEAVE SO FAST, BUT CHAOS IS RUNNING RAMPANT ALL OVER THE GLOBE.
STAGGOIL
APPRECIATE THE HELP, BUT YOU'RE TOO LATE, SUPERMAN.
THIS OIL SPILL IS SO CATASTROPHIC, IT'LL BE FELT FOR YEARS.
MORE THAN I CAN KEEP UP WITH.
CHECK IT OUT! THE MAN SHOWED UP TO HELP THE GUARDS!
WE OUTNUMBER HIM!
TAKE HIM!
BACK IN YOUR CELLS.
THIS IS YOUR LAST WARNING.
I'VE SEEN SIMILAR ERUPTIONS BEFORE, BUT NEVER WITH THIS LEVEL OF ANIMOSITY AND VINDICTIVENESS.
WHAT DO YOU CARE IF I TORCH THESE ONE-PERCENTERS' MANSIONS?
THEY'RE STEALIN' FROM US! THEY DESERVE TO SUFFER!
SOMETHING MORE... SOMETHING DARKER IS AT WORK HERE.
AS THOUGH ANGER AND IGNORANCE HAVE BOILED OVER ALL AT ONCE.
WHERE PEOPLE CAN'T LOOK PAST THEIR OWN SELFISHNESS...
...AND THE COMMON GOOD IS A FOREIGN CONCEPT.
NO.

LOGAMBA.
I LEFT THE VACCINE AT THIS VERY CAMP JUST A SHORT TIME AGO!
NOW MEN, WOMEN, CHILDREN...EVEN DOCTORS...
DEAD.
WHY?
WHO WOULD--?
Uhnn...
WHAT HAPPENED HERE?
GUERILLAS...
REEEOWWWWW
HANG ON. I'LL GET YOU TO A HOSPITAL.
TOOK IT ALL...
STAY WITH ME!
IS THAT--?
WHAKOOM

I COULDN'T SAVE HER!
I COULDN'T--!
WHO DID THIS?!
THAT VILLAGE THE GUERRILLAS MIGHT BE HIDING IN? PARTS OF IT STILL STAND.
FLATTEN IT BEFORE WE GIVE AWAY OUR POSITION.
LEAVE NOTHING.
YOUR OWN PEOPLE?!
WHAT'S WRONG WITH YOU?!
KRAMMM
MORTARS!
THE GUERRILLAS FOUND US!
GET BA--
WHOOM

WHY?
WHY WOULD YOU DO THIS TO EACH OTHER?
BECAUSE THEY ARE PETTY.
SELF-OBSESSED.
INCAPABLE OF LOOKING PAST THEMSELVES TO CARE FOR ONE ANOTHER.
YOU SHOULD HAVE REALIZED THAT BY NOW.
THESE PEOPLE DON'T DESERVE YOU.
THEY HAVEN'T SINCE THE MOMENT YOU ARRIVED.
YOU!
OZ.
THE TIME HAS COME FOR US TO TALK.
NOT HERE.
SOMEWHERE...

...SAFE.
MORE SUITABLE.
MY FORTRESS. HOW DID YOU--?
I HAVE BEEN HERE BEFORE, AFTER ALL.
YOU'RE RESPONSIBLE FOR GLOBAL CHAOS?
I DID NOTHING BUT PRESENT THEM WITH OPTIONS.
THEY HAD A CHOICE BETWEEN DARKNESS AND LIGHT.
DARKNESS WON.
THEY EMBRACED MURDER, MAYHEM AND DESTRUCTION.
YOU CALLED THEM HUMANS. YOU AREN'T--?
OF EARTH? NO.
HAD I ONLY KNOWN WHAT A CESSPOOL THIS PLACE IS, I'D HAVE SENT YOU SOMEWHERE BETTER.
"SENT"?
WHAT ARE YOU TALKING ABOUT?
WHO ARE YOU?
I FASHIONED THE SPACECRAFT THAT ENABLED YOU TO ESCAPE KRYPTON'S DEMISE.
I SENT YOU HERE, KAL.
YOU CAN'T...
...POSSIBLY...
...MEAN...
I MEAN EXACTLY THAT.

I SURVIVED, KAL-EL.
AND I KNOW NOW THAT I SENT YOU TO THE WRONG PLACE.
I AM YOUR FATHER.
I AM...
...JOR-EL.

ROBSON
DANIEL
WRIGHT

ROBSON
DANIEL
WRIGHT

LIAR.

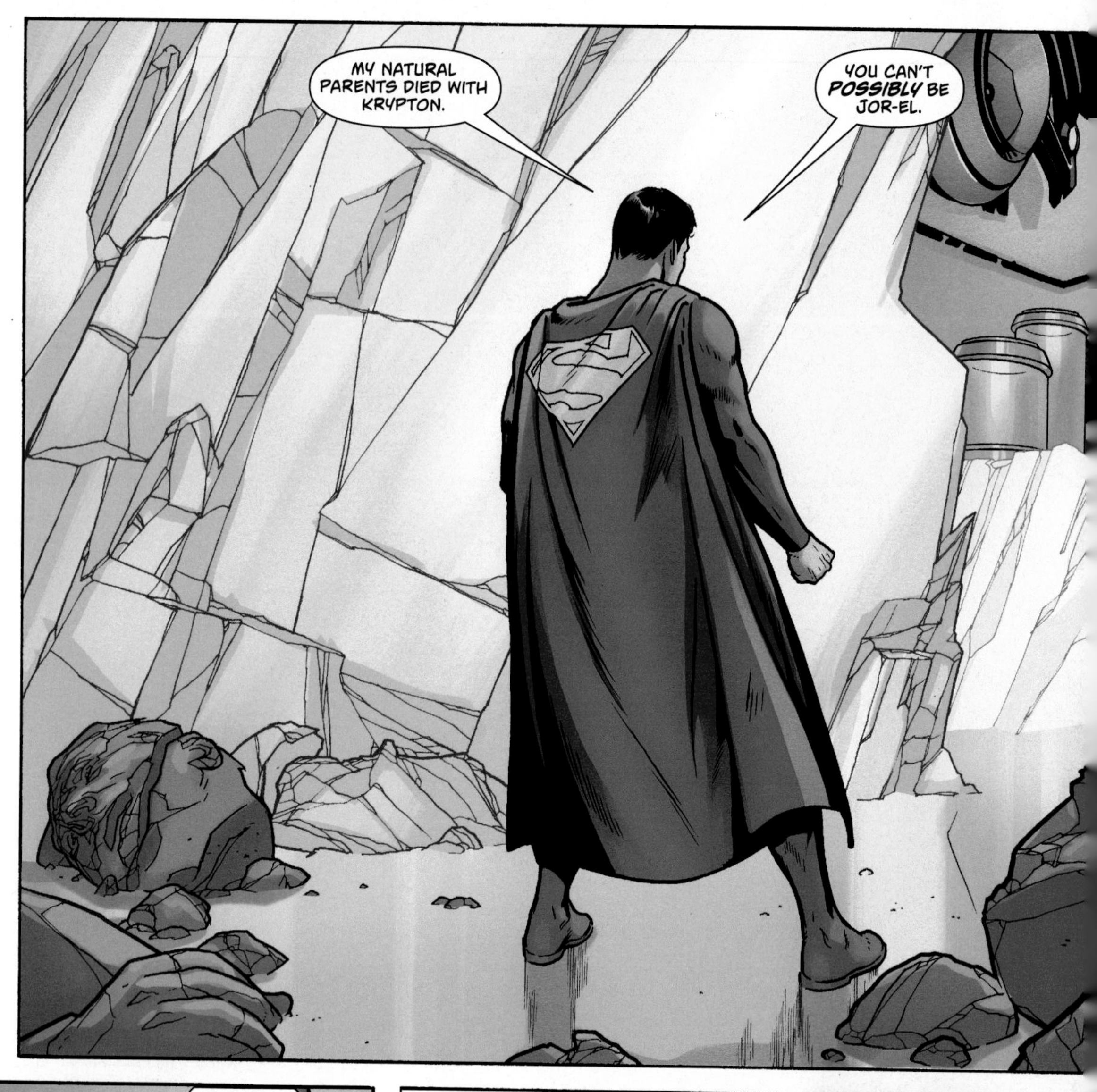
MY NATURAL PARENTS DIED WITH KRYPTON.
YOU CAN'T *POSSIBLY* BE JOR-EL.

I *AM* YOUR *FATHER.*

FULL-SPECTRUM ANALYSIS, *KELEX.*
THE *WORKS.*
IDENTIFY THIS FRAUD.

I UNDERSTAND YOUR DOUBT, KAL.
DESPITE YOUR SKEPTICISM, I ASK THAT YOU LISTEN TO MY STORY, FOR I SPEAK THE *TRUTH*.
KRYPTON *DIED*.
BUT I *SURVIVED*.

KELEX WILL DO WHAT YOU SAY, BUT NOT UNTIL *I* ASK.
AFTER ALL, HE IS PROGRAMMED TO RESPOND TO HIS INVENTOR FIRST...
SIR.

...AND HIS INVENTOR'S PROGENY *SECOND*.
FULFILL HIS REQUEST, KELEX.
YES, SIR.

DNA SENSORS, RETINA SCAN AND VOICE ANALYSIS ARE *CONCLUSIVE*.

THE OZ EFFECT
PART TWO
DAN JURGENS WRITER RYAN SOOK ART
MAY I PRESENT YOUR FATHER.
JOR-EL OF KRYPTON.
HI-FI COLOR ROB LEIGH LETTERS
ROBSON ROCHA, DANIEL HENRIQUES & JASON WRIGHT COVER
NEIL EDWARDS & JEROMY COX VARIANT COVER
ANDREA SHEA ASSISTANT EDITOR
MIKE COTTON & PAUL KAMINSKI EDITORS
EDDIE BERGANZA GROUP EDITOR
SUPERMAN created by JERRY SIEGEL and JOE SHUSTER. BY SPECIAL ARRANGEMENT WITH THE JERRY SIEGEL FAMILY.

NO.
IT'S A TRICK.
LIKE WHEN MXYZPTLK PASSED HIMSELF OFF AS CLARK KENT.*
*SUPERMAN REBORN. --Paul & Cotton

THEN HOW DID I KNOW WHERE TO FIND YOU WHEN WE FIRST MET?
OR KNOW TO BRING YOU HERE?

YOUR BOY IS GROWING UP FAST. YOU AND LOIS MUST BE PROUD.
THE MOTEL...*
FRIEND OR ENEMY IS TOO SIMPLE A TERM WHEN YOU CONSIDER THE LONG GAME.
*DC UNIVERSE: REBIRTH. --P & C

I HAVE BEEN WATCHING YOU ALL YOUR LIFE. MY GRANDSON AS WELL.
I STILL DON'T--!
HOW DID YOU--?

AMONG THEIR MANY FUNCTIONS, THESE CRYSTALS SERVE TO ARCHIVE OUR HOUSE'S HISTORY.
YOUR EXPERIENCES AND MEMORIES...
...AS WELL AS MINE.

LET US LOOK INTO THE PAST, WHEN I FOUGHT FOR KRYPTON'S FUTURE WITH THE SAME FERVOR AND DEDICATION YOU APPLY TO EARTH'S.
WE'RE GOING BACK...
TO A HAPPIER TIME.
OUR CONSCIOUSNESS WILL BE INSERTED INTO OUR ARCHIVED HISTORY.

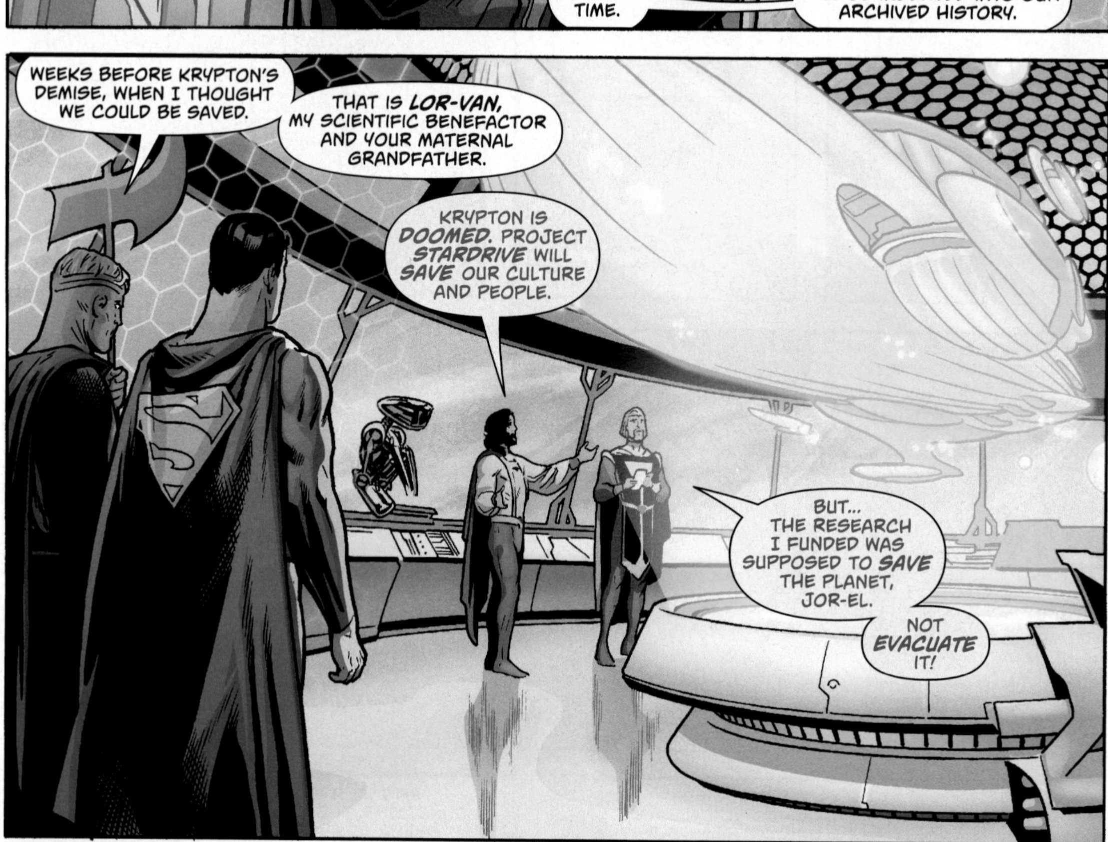
WEEKS BEFORE KRYPTON'S DEMISE, WHEN I THOUGHT WE COULD BE SAVED.
THAT IS *LOR-VAN,* MY SCIENTIFIC BENEFACTOR AND YOUR MATERNAL GRANDFATHER.
KRYPTON IS *DOOMED.* PROJECT *STARDRIVE* WILL *SAVE* OUR CULTURE AND PEOPLE.
BUT... THE RESEARCH I FUNDED WAS SUPPOSED TO *SAVE* THE PLANET, JOR-EL.
NOT *EVACUATE* IT!

SAVING KRYPTON IS *IMPOSSIBLE.* I REALIZE THAT SPACE TRAVEL IS FORBIDDEN, BUT--
DEEMED ILLEGAL BECAUSE OF JAX-UR'S *CRIMES!*
AS THE PLANET'S LAST ASTRONAUT, I KNOW FULL WELL THAT THIS RESEARCH IS *FORBIDDEN.*

SAVING LIVES IS *NEVER* WRONG!
I'M PROVIDING *HOPE!*

THAT'S--!
YOUR BEAUTIFUL MOTHER, LARA, DAYS BEFORE YOUR BIRTH.
PLEASE. AT THIS TIME, ABOVE ALL OTHERS...
...I WANT THE TWO MOST IMPORTANT MEN IN MY LIFE TO GET ALONG.

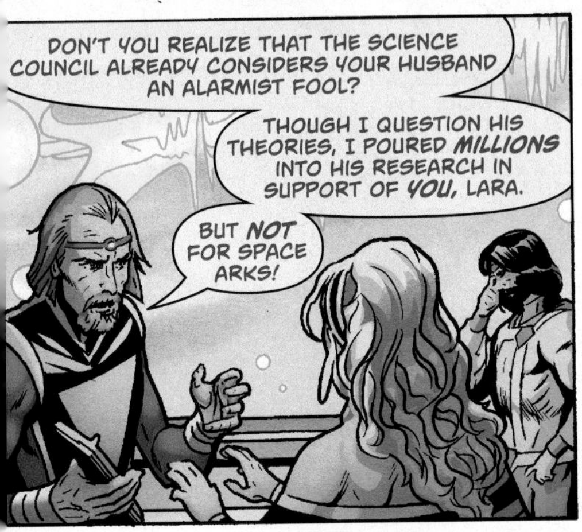
DON'T YOU REALIZE THAT THE SCIENCE COUNCIL ALREADY CONSIDERS YOUR HUSBAND AN ALARMIST FOOL?
THOUGH I QUESTION HIS THEORIES, I POURED MILLIONS INTO HIS RESEARCH IN SUPPORT OF YOU, LARA.
BUT NOT FOR SPACE ARKS!

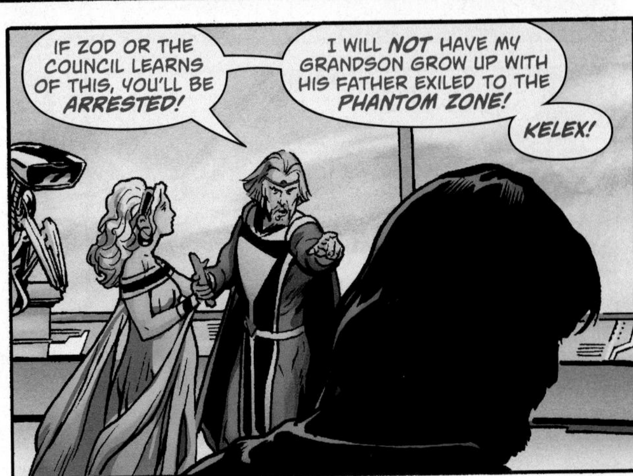
IF ZOD OR THE COUNCIL LEARNS OF THIS, YOU'LL BE ARRESTED!
I WILL NOT HAVE MY GRANDSON GROW UP WITH HIS FATHER EXILED TO THE PHANTOM ZONE!
KELEX!

I FUNDED YOUR DEVELOPMENT, SO YOU WILL RESPOND TO MY COMMANDS.
ERASE ALL OF THIS!
DESTROY EVERY BIT OF DATA ON PROJECT STARDRIVE!
DONE.

FATHER--?!
MY OWN GRANDFATHER DID THAT?
THE FIRST TIME I WAS BETRAYED.
IT WOULD NOT BE THE LAST.

YOU'LL THANK ME ONE DAY.
WHEN YOU'VE DOOMED ALL OF US?
NEVER!

THIS REALLY HAPPENED?
IT WAS NEVER AS SIMPLE AS THE SCIENCE COUNCIL REJECTING MY RESEARCH.
COUNTLESS WRONGS CONTRIBUTED TO OUR DESTRUCTION.

THEY ERASED MY DATA, BUT NOT MY MEMORY.
I REPROGRAMMED KELEX TO FOLLOW MY COMMANDS AND REBUILT WHAT I COULD.
NO ARMADA. JUST ONE SMALL SHIP.
HE WILL CARRY THE HISTORY, THOUGHTS AND DREAMS OF KRYPTON WITH HIM.

OUR LAST SHARED EXPERIENCE, KAL.
BUT, AS KRYPTON DIED, WE TOOK SOLACE IN KNOWING...

"...THAT YOU WERE TRAVELING TO A WORLD THAT WOULD WELCOME YOU WITH OPEN ARMS.
"ALL WE HOPED FOR WAS A QUICK, PAINLESS END.

"BUT THAT WAS NOT TO BE.
"ON THE VERGE OF DEATH...

"...IN THE SMALLEST INCREMENT OF TIME POSSIBLE, SOMETHING INTERVENED.
"IN A MOMENT FAR MORE HORRIFYING AND PAINFUL THAN ANYTHING I COULD IMAGINE...

"...I WATCHED YOUR MOTHER DIE.
"WHILE I LIVED."

THIS GOES AGAINST EVERYTHING I'VE EVER KNOWN.
THE CRYSTALS ON YOUR SHIP RECEIVED DATA UP TO THE MOMENT OF YOUR DEPARTURE.
THEY RECORDED KRYPTON'S DEMISE, NEVER KNOWING THAT FOR ME...

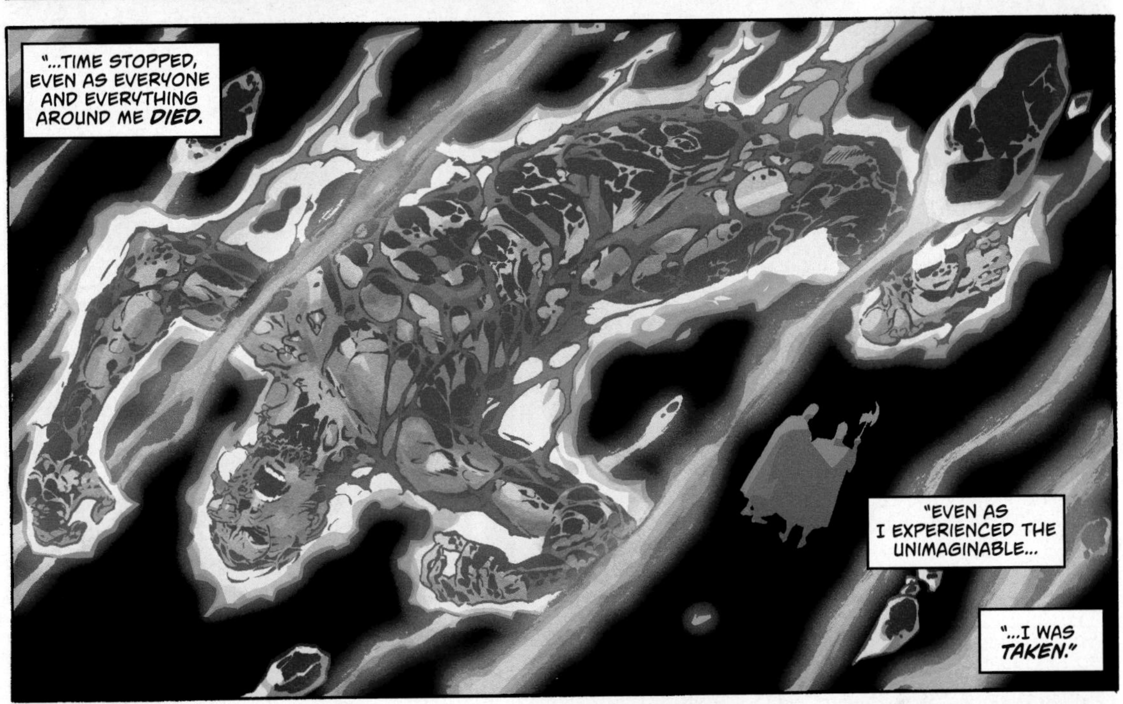
"...TIME STOPPED, EVEN AS EVERYONE AND EVERYTHING AROUND ME DIED.
"EVEN AS I EXPERIENCED THE UNIMAGINABLE...
"...I WAS TAKEN."

WHO COULD POSSIBLY--?
SOMETHING BEYOND US.
A BEING ABLE TO BEND REALITY TO HIS EVERY WHIM, THOUGH I DIDN'T WANT IT.

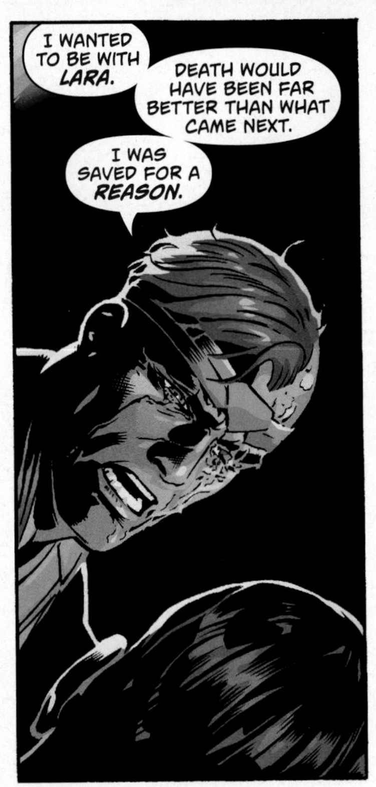
I WANTED TO BE WITH LARA.
DEATH WOULD HAVE BEEN FAR BETTER THAN WHAT CAME NEXT.
I WAS SAVED FOR A REASON.

WHY?
I THINK... I WAS SAVED TO BEAR WITNESS TO THE TRUTH.

WHAT TRUTH?
EARTH'S.
THE NATURE OF ITS PEOPLE AND WHAT THEY REALLY ARE.

IF YOU'RE REALLY WHO YOU CLAIM--
YOU STILL DON'T BELIEVE ME?

I WANT TO.
BUT...
...I'VE BEEN DECEIVED BEFORE.

THIS ALL SEEMS SO IMPOSSIBLE--WITH SO MANY UNANSWERED QUESTIONS.
SUCH AS HOW DID I, LIKE YOU, END UP ON EARTH?
YOU ARRIVED TO FIND SAFETY IN THE LOVING EMBRACE OF THE KENTS.

THE LIGHT THAT SAVED ME CARRIED ME TO A VERY DIFFERENT PLACE.
THE MOST LAWLESS, DANGEROUS CITY EARTH HAD TO OFFER.
⟨IS HE ALIVE?⟩
⟨I THINK HE'S AN AMERICAN?⟩
⟨LOOK FOR MONEY!⟩
⟨NO.⟩

⟨WE WILL HELP THE POOR MAN.⟩
⟨HELP HIM? WE SHOULD TURN HIM OVER TO KASSAM.⟩

⟨SO THAT BUTCHER CAN TORTURE HIM, HOLD HIM FOR RANSOM...⟩
⟨...OR SIMPLY KILL HIM?⟩
⟨NO.⟩
⟨IT IS RIGHTEOUS TO HELP THE WAYFARER.⟩

⟨WON'T KASSAM PUNISH US IF WE SAY NOTHING, MOTHER?⟩
⟨THE STRANGER DOES NOT NEED A GUN IN HIS FACE, AAZIM.⟩
⟨HE NEEDS HELP.⟩
⟨THESE STRANGE, GREEN SPLINTERS. I DARE REMOVE NO MORE.⟩

THE CITY MIGHT HAVE BEEN WAR-TORN, BUT THEY CARED FOR YOU.
SO THEY DID. NOT THAT I WANTED IT, KAL.
AT THE TIME, I WAS A DAMAGED, EMOTIONALLY EMPTY MAN.

"BUT SOMETHING WANTED ME ALIVE TO SEE HUMANITY FOR WHAT IT REALLY IS."
⟨I REGRET I CANNOT OFFER MORE, BUT FOOD IS SCARCE.⟩

LEAVE ME ALONE!
"I DIDN'T CARE IF I LIVED.
"AT LEAST NOT UNTIL A YOUNG BOY..."

⟨BUT I AM HUNGRY.⟩
⟨OUR HONORED GUEST WILL EAT FIRST, AAZIM.⟩
"HE MADE ME THINK OF YOU, KAL."

"I DIDN'T KNOW YOUR FATE. WERE YOU IN A HELLHOLE LIKE ME?
"OR WORSE?"
<GO. YOU MUST HIDE DURING THE DAY.>

"I COULDN'T GO OUT TO FEEL THE SUN ON MY FACE.
"I SPENT DAYS IN THE DARK, THINKING ABOUT WHAT COULD HAVE BEEN.
"I WAS ALONE.

"UNTIL..."
KASSAM'S ARMY NEEDS FOOD!
NOW!
"IN THE MIDST OF A CIVIL WAR, FOOD HAD BECOME A WEAPON.
"STARVATION, A TACTIC."

<DID YOU SEE THEIR GUNS? THAT'S WHAT MAKES THEM POWERFUL!>
<THEY LEFT NOTHING! IT'S ALL WE HAD!>

"I CONTINUED TO HEAL IN THE MIDST OF SCREAMS, GUNFIRE AND BODIES ROTTING IN THE STREETS.
"DEATH WAS EVERYWHERE.
"I COULDN'T STOP WORRYING ABOUT YOU."

‹FOOD IS NOW PRECIOUS AND YOUR PRESENCE ENDANGERS MY FAMILY.›
‹YOU ARE HEALED ENOUGH TO TRAVEL.›
‹PLEASE, YOU MUST *LEAVE.*›

‹IF YOU DON'T, I WILL TURN YOU OVER TO KASSAM AND GAIN HIS FAVOR.›
‹WE WOULD NOT GO TO BED HUNGRY AGAIN.›
"I REALIZED THAT I OWED THEM.

"THAT NIGHT, I DECIDED TO REPAY THEIR KINDNESS.
"SNEAKING INTO THE WARLORD'S CAMP WAS EASY.
"THEY HAD NO IDEA ANYONE WOULD DARE DO SUCH A THING."

‹I FORGOT HOW GOOD ACTUAL *MEAT* TASTES!›
"I THINK BY HELPING THAT FAMILY, IN A WAY...I FELT AS THOUGH I WAS HELPING *YOU.*"
‹HOW DID YOU COME TO POSSESS IT, STRANGER?›

‹I STOLE FROM KASSAM, AAZ.›

"I WAS WRONG."
‹THE BOY INSISTS ON SPEAKING WITH YOU, KASSAM.›
‹*WELL?*›

‹THERE IS SOMETHING YOU MUST KNOW, SIR.›
‹SOMETHING *IMPORTANT.*›

BRAKKKT
"ALL I WANTED WAS TO FEED A HUNGRY FAMILY.
"THE IDEA THAT SOMEONE COULD BE SO EVIL AS TO DENY A HUMAN BEING FOOD...

...WAS COMPLETELY FOREIGN TO ME.
I COULD NOT FATHOM THE CONSEQUENCES TO COME.
‹STEAL FROM ME...›
‹...AND YOU PAY.›
CRACK

‹DON'T HURT THE BOY!›

‹HURT HIM?›
"AS THE SUN ROSE, I WAS TOO PREOCCUPIED TO REALIZE THAT THE KICK DIDN'T HURT."
THAK

‹I WILL REWARD HIM!›

‹YOU CAN BE **ONE** OF US, YOUNG ONE.›
‹BE ONE WHO RULES THIS FORSAKEN PLACE.›
‹TO EARN THAT EXALTED POSITION, YOU MUST **PUNISH** THE TRAITORS.›
‹**ALL OF THEM.**›

‹BUT...›

‹DON'T **DO THIS,** AAZ!›
‹**DON'T!**›

‹YOU **KNOW** THEY VIOLATED MY LAW.›
‹**PROVE** YOU DESERVE TO **JOIN US.**›
‹I **CAN'T!**›

‹**YES...**›

‹...YOU **CAN.**›
RATT

MY GOD.
THERE WAS NO GOD PRESENT THAT DAY.
ONLY MAN'S CAPACITY FOR EVIL.

HA HAHH!

‹YOUR TURN.›
KLIK
‹HOW...›
‹...COULD YOU DO THIS?›

"TO THIS DAY, I DON'T KNOW IF IT WAS AS SIMPLE AS BEING IN THE SUN...

"...OR IF MY CONTROLLER LET MY POWERS EMERGE.
"IN MY RAGE, I COULD NOT HOLD BACK."

‹WHY, AAZIM?›

WHY?!

"THAT'S WHEN I KNEW HUMANITY WAS *HOPELESS*.
"THAT THERE IS NO SAVING THEM FROM THEMSELVES.
BRATTA BRAT

"WITH THAT REALIZATION, I WAS TAKEN AGAIN."
10

THAT WAS *AWFUL*, I ADMIT.
BUT THAT HARDLY REPRESENTS ALL OF HUMANITY.
I WARNED KRYPTON.

THEY DID NOT LISTEN.

JUST AS EARTHERS WILL *NEVER* LISTEN TO YOU.
YOU CAN'T USE ONE TERRIBLE EVENT AS--

I EXPERIENCED *FAR* MORE THAN JUST ONE EVENT.

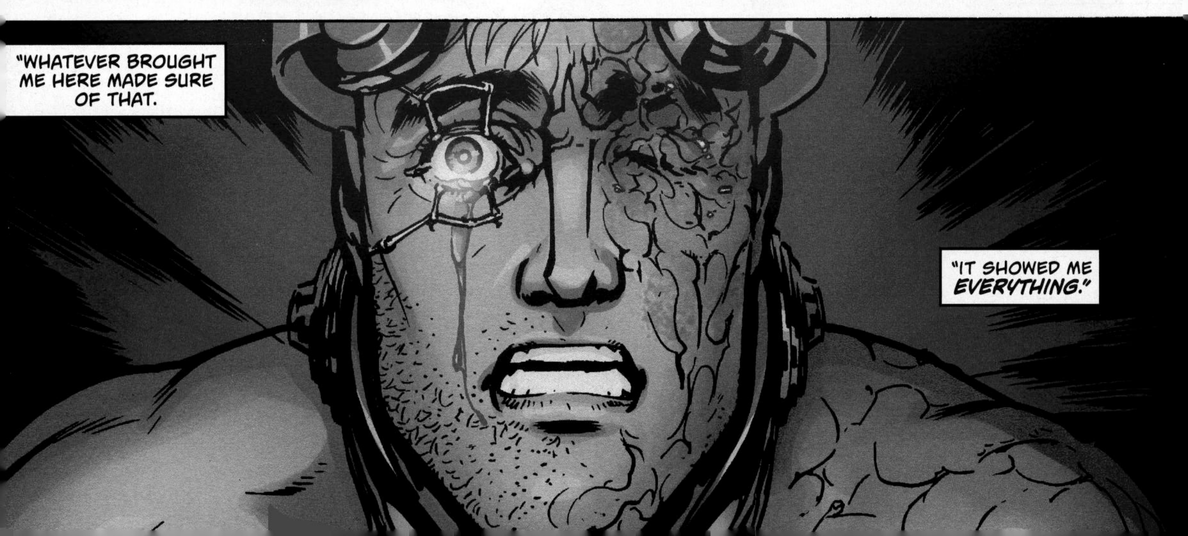
"WHATEVER BROUGHT ME HERE MADE SURE OF THAT.
"IT SHOWED ME *EVERYTHING*."

"THE HISTORY OF MAN.
"A NEVER-ENDING CASCADE OF HEINOUS ATROCITIES, ONE AFTER ANOTHER.
"CENTURIES, DECADES AND YEARS UNFOLDED, WITH NOTHING CHANGING.
"NOTHING IMPROVING.
"IF ANYTHING, TECHNOLOGY ALLOWED MAN TO BECOME A MORE EFFICIENT KILLER...
"...AS HIS CAPACITY FOR CRUELTY INCREASED.
"THERE, BEYOND THE CONFINES OF TIME AND SPACE, I LEARNED, BEYOND A SHADOW OF A DOUBT, THAT THESE PEOPLE ARE HOPELESS.
"THEY SIMPLY DO NOT DESERVE YOU."

THEY CLAIM BENEVOLENCE AS THEY ADVOCATE SEEMINGLY OBVIOUS IDEALS, BUT IN REALITY ARE UNENLIGHTENED SAVAGES.
CONQUEST, MATERIAL GAIN, SUBJUGATION AND SELF-INTEREST WILL FOREVER LIMIT THEM.
TRAITS SUCH AS THESE DOOMED KRYPTON.
BUT THESE PEOPLE OF YOURS...

...ARE WORSE.
THEY DESERVE WHAT'S COMING.
HAD I KNOWN THEY'D FOREVER IGNORE THE INSPIRATION YOU PROVIDE...
...I WOULD NOT HAVE SENT YOU HERE.
THEIR PEOPLE ARE SO MIRED IN THE ETERNAL DESPAIR OF THEIR OWN CREATION...

...THAT I AM SOMEWHAT AMAZED--AND PROUD--THAT YOU GREW TO BECOME THE MAN YOU ARE TODAY.
YOU'RE WRONG. I ALWAYS HAVE HOPE THAT--

OF COURSE YOU DO. JUST AS I HAD HOPE FOR KRYPTON.
LOOK WHERE IT GOT ME.

WHY NOW? WHAT ARE YOU TRYING TO SAY?

I MADE A GRAVE MISTAKE IN SENDING YOU HERE, SON.
FOR WHICH I AM SORRY.

EARTH'S FATE IS SEALED.
THERE IS NO MORE TIME.
THESE LOST SOULS DON'T DESERVE ANOTHER SECOND OF YOUR LIFE.
GATHER YOUR THINGS.
I'M TAKING YOU AWAY FROM HERE...
...FOREVER.

after Quitely

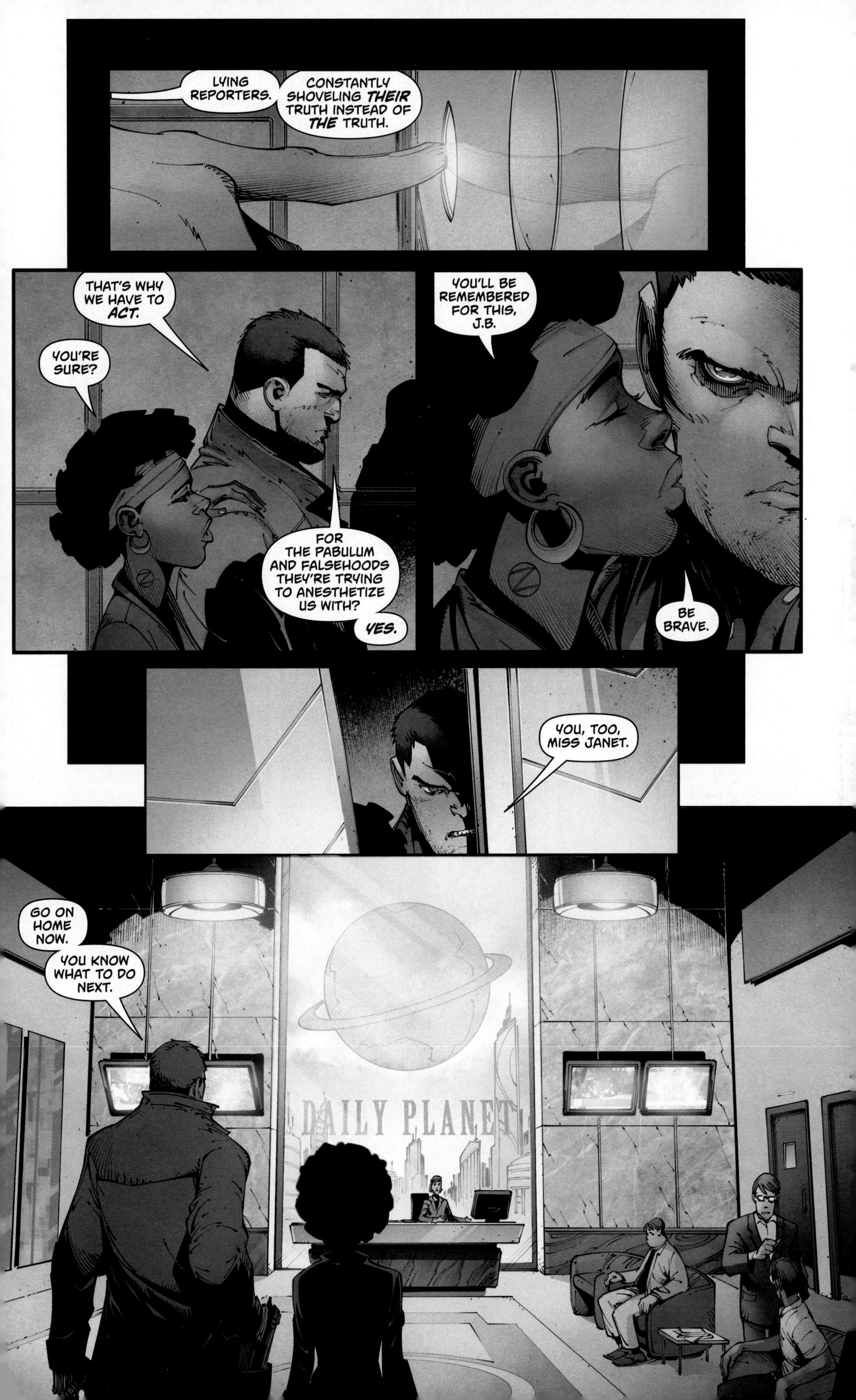
LYING REPORTERS.
CONSTANTLY SHOVELING THEIR TRUTH INSTEAD OF THE TRUTH.
THAT'S WHY WE HAVE TO ACT.
YOU'RE SURE?
FOR THE PABULUM AND FALSEHOODS THEY'RE TRYING TO ANESTHETIZE US WITH?
YES.
YOU'LL BE REMEMBERED FOR THIS, J.B.
BE BRAVE.
YOU, TOO, MISS JANET.
GO ON HOME NOW.
YOU KNOW WHAT TO DO NEXT.
DAILY PLANET

...NUCLEAR POWER PLANT SABOTAGED...
...CHILD BEATEN TO DEATH FOR LUNCH MONEY...
BREAKING NEWS TRAGIC DEATH
4
SO MANY THINGS HAPPENING AT ONCE. LIKE THE WORLD IS COMING UNGLUED.
COINCIDENCE... OR IS SOMETHING BIGGER GOING ON?
LEVEL SEVEN SCORE.
...AFTERNOON OF TERROR IN A HOSPITAL AS...

WHERE'S SUPERMAN IN ALL OF THIS, CHIEF?
JIMMY, IF I KNOW HIM, I'LL BET HE'S RALLYING THE LEAGUE TO--
PLEASE DON'T--!

POK POK POK
GUNSHOTS?!
TAKE JON AND HEAD FOR THE BACK STAIRS, LOIS!
JON! GET OVER HERE BEFORE--

OH MY GOD!
BRAMM

THAT'S RIGHT. WE'RE ALL GOIN' TO SEE GOD.
TOGETHER.
"EARTH WILL DESTROY ITSELF, KAL."

YOU CLAIM TO BE MY FATHER-- JOR-EL.
MAYBE... AND JUST MAYBE... THAT'S TRUE.
BUT IF YOU THINK I'M GOING TO TAKE MY FAMILY AND LEAVE EARTH...
...YOU'RE CRAZY.
THEY DON'T DESERVE YOU.
I AM YOUR FATHER, SON.
I KNOW THESE EARTHERS-- SHORTCOMINGS AND ALL--FAR TOO WELL.
ABANDON THIS WORLD WHILE YOU CAN.
IF YOU'VE REALLY BEEN WATCHING ME ALL MY LIFE, THEN YOU KNOW I DON'T RUN FROM ANYTHING. LEAST OF ALL...
...FROM HELPING PEOPLE.
HUMAN BEINGS AREN'T PERFECT.
BUT I'VE ALWAYS SEEN IT AS MY JOB TO HELP SHOW THEM THE WAY.
I TRY TO PROVIDE HOPE AND INSPIRATION SO THAT WE ALL GET BETTER, A LITTLE BIT AT A TIME.
DESPITE THEIR PROPENSITY FOR VIOLENCE? GENOCIDE?
YOU, OF ALL PEOPLE, SHOULD BE AWARE OF THE ABUSE THEY INFLICT ON THEMSELVES AND THEIR WORLD!
AT THIS VERY MOMENT, CHAOS IS RUNNING RAMPANT ACROSS THE GLOBE.
HUMANITY IS BEYOND SAVING.
SHOW HIM, KELEX.
ACCESSING NEWS OUTLETS AND PRIVATE NETWORKS NOW.
A CROSS SECTION OF HUMANITY, KAL-EL.
MY--

DAN JURGENS STORY & BREAKDOWN ART VIKTOR BOGDANOVIC PENCILS
PART II
--GOD.
BOGDANOVIC & TREVOR SCOTT INKS
MIKE SPICER COLOR ROB LEIGH LETTERS
NICK BRADSHAW & BRAD ANDERSON COVER
NEIL EDWARDS & JEROMY COX VARIANT CO
ANDREA SHEA ASST. EDITOR PAUL KAMINSKI & MIKE COTTON EDIT
EDDIE BERGANZA GROUP EDI
SUPERMAN created by JERRY SIEGEL and JOE SHUSTER. SUPERBOY created by JERRY SIEGEL. BY SPECIAL ARRANGEMENT WITH THE JERRY SIEGEL FAM

I HAVE TO GO.
WHY BOTHER?
THESE PEOPLE ARE A VICIOUS, NEVER-ENDING CYCLE, KAL.
IT'S WHO THEY ARE.
I'M NEEDED.
THEY'LL ALWAYS NEED YOU.
THEY ARE INCAPABLE OF OVERCOMING THEMSELVES.
I HAVE JUST RECEIVED REPORTS OF CHEMICAL WEAPONS BEING USED IN LOGAMBA'S CIVIL WAR.
BECAUSE YOU TOOK ME AWAY FROM THERE.
I WILL NEVER ABANDON EARTH...
...AND THERE'S NOTHING YOU CAN DO TO CHANGE THAT!
DO NOT BE SO SURE OF THAT, MY SON.
EVENTS IN LOGAMBA ARE PROCEEDING EVEN FASTER THAN YOUR AGENTS PREDICTED, SIR.

METROPOLIS.
PLEASE. RATHER THAN RESORT TO VIOLENCE, TELL ME WHAT YOUR PROBLEMS WITH THE DAILY PLANET ARE...
...AND WE'LL FIX THEM. TOGETHER.
HAVE TO BUY TIME.
HOPE THAT CLARK FIGURES OUT WHAT'S HAPPENING.

AND GETS HERE BEFORE IT'S TOO LATE.
YOU CAN'T TAKE BACK YOUR LIES!
THE WORLD MUST KNOW THAT YOU PRINT FAKE NEWS IN ORDER TO CONTROL US!

BULL!
IF THERE'S ANYTHING THIS PAPER AND I STAND FOR--IT'S THE TRUTH!
THAT'S A LIE AND YOU KNOW IT!
LET ME TELL YOUR SIDE OF THE STORY. I WANT TO HELP YOU.

I KNOW THE TRUTH. OZ SHOWED US WHAT'S REAL.
THAT YOU'RE HIDING THE TRUTH OF HOW BAD THINGS ARE.
OZ?
CLARK TOLD ME OZ COULD BE A THREAT, BUT WE HAD NO IDEA HE HAD FOLLOWERS.

OZ UNDERSTANDS.
KNOWS THAT FOR MOST--THERE IS NO TOMORROW.
BUDDY, THE ONLY THING I KNOW...

IS THAT
OU'RE A
LOSER.
AN' IF THERE'S ANYTHING I CAN'T STAND--IT'S LOSING.
STEVE?!
POK POK POK
BACK OFF, HAS-BEEN.
GUH--!
WE WILL NOT BE DETERRED!
I NEED A KEYBOARD.
CLARK ALWAYS SAID THAT IF ANYTHING GOT OUT OF HAND I SHOULD SEND WORD TO THE FORTRESS.
STOP THIS!
NO MATTER WHERE HE IS, KELEX CAN FIND AND ALERT HIM.
WE HAVE A CHILD HERE!
DETONATE THAT BOMB NOW AND NO ONE WILL HEAR WHAT YOU HAVE TO SAY!
I'M LOIS LANE AND MY REPUTATION IS AS GOOD AS IT GETS.
LET ME TELL YOUR STORY, WORD FOR WORD.
TRUST ME.

BUT FIRST YOU HAVE TO LET THESE PEOPLE GO.
THEN I'LL TYPE WHATEVER YOU WANT, WORD FOR WORD, AND UPLOAD IT TO OUR SITE.
WHAT IF I STILL WANT TO PRESS THE BUTTON AFTER THAT?
I PRAY YOU WON'T...
...BUT I WOULDN'T BE ABLE TO STOP YOU.
MOM--?
IT'LL BE OKAY, JON. JUST GIVE THIS MAN AND ME A LITTLE... SOLITUDE.
LET PEOPLE SEE THEIR CRAP LIVES REALLY BUST LOOSE.
GET HONEST. RAZE AND BURN CITIES.
I LIKE IT.
"YOU GOT A DEAL, LANE. THE REST OF YOU...MOVE OUT."
I NOTIFIED HIS EXCELLENCY THAT THE MISSILES WERE LOADED AND READY.
HE GAVE THE LAUNCH ORDER.
HE'D USE CHEMICAL WEAPONS AGAINST HIS OWN PEOPLE?
FIRE!
CHOOM
CHOOM
CHOOM
THE THRONE MUST BE PROTECTED FROM THOSE SAVAGE BUTCHERS.
THE ONLY BUTCHER I SEE HERE...

...IS YOU.
WHOOOM
BRAMM
THAT TAKES CARE OF THE LAUNCHERS.
NOW FOR THE MISSILES.

WE CAN'T LEAVE, UNCLE PERRY!
MOM NEEDS US!
DAILY PLAN
YOUR MOM IS THE SMARTEST, MOST CAPABLE PERSON I KNOW, JON.
SHE'LL BE FINE.
BELIEVE IT.

THERE. EVERYTHING YOU'VE SAID IS ON OUR SITE, WORD FOR WORD.
I'M NOT DONE. KEEP TYPING.
WATCHING ME LIKE A HAWK.
NEED HIM TO TURN AWAY... JUST FOR A SECOND.
I'M CONFUSED. WHAT CAN YOU POSSIBLY HOPE TO GAIN BY INCITING MASS VIOLENCE?
THE END IS COMING, LADY.
OZ WILL SURVIVE.
AND MAYBE HE'LL TAKE THE PEOPLE WHO REALLY UNDERSTAND THINGS WITH HIM.
HEY, DID I JUST HEAR--?
NOW'S MY CHANCE.
FIND HIM, KELEX. FAST.
PEOPLE ARE ALWAYS PREDICTING THE END OF THE WORLD. IT NEVER--
LIAR!
THIS TIME IT WILL!
I KNOW I DON'T STAND A CHANCE, BUT I'LL MAKE IT SO MY JANET DOES!
BAMM
BAM
GUNSHOTS?!
LOOK! IT'S D--
--SUPERMAN!

SKASSSH
THIS HAPPENS RIGHT--
SUPERMAN!

--GUH!--
BBAK

BWHOOM
SKASH

HELLO, LOIS.

YOU'RE NOT SUPERMAN...
...WHO...
OH.

...MARTIAL LAW DECLARED IN ATHENS...
...THOUSANDS OF CIVILIAN CASUALTIES...
...MASS STARVATION...
I AM HIS FATHER, LOIS.
I AM JOR-EL.
BLOODY RIOTS
WAR
LIVE FAMI E

DID YOU SEE THAT?!
THAT MEANS LOIS IS OKAY, RIGHT?
SEE, JON? YOUR MOM IS JUST FI--!
--JON?

MOM WOULDN'T WANT ME TO DUCK OUT ON UNCLE PERRY LIKE THAT...
...BUT SHE'D LIKE IT EVEN LESS IF HE SAW ME DOIN' THIS.
AND NOW THAT DAD IS HERE AND THE BUILDING IS EMPTY...
...THE COAST IS CLEAR FOR
SUPERBOY
TO HELP!
ONLY TWO LEFT.
CAN'T JUST KNOCK THEM OUT OF THE SKY.
CHEMICAL WEAPONS NEED SPECIAL CARE.

THE RESERVOIR TANK.
KRIPP

HAVE TO MAKE SURE THE GAS CAN'T ESCAPE.
TSSS

SO THAT NO ONE ELSE USES IT.
EVER.

BAD ENOUGH THE GOVERNMENT USES SUCH A HEINOUS TACTIC.
BUT THE REBELS ARE USING INNOCENT CIVILIANS AS SHIELDS.

MAKES ME WONDER IF JOR-EL--IF THAT'S WHO HE REALLY IS--
--IS RIGHT.

IS HUMANITY BEYOND SALVATION?
NO.
THAT IS A CHEMICAL ROCKET!
THE ROYAL FAMILY WOULD REALLY DO THAT TO US?
THAT PROVES THEY MUST DIE!
I WON'T ACCEPT THAT.
EVER.
THERE HAS TO BE HOPE FOR US OR--
BWHOOM
THEY DON'T REALIZE WE ROBBED THEIR ARMORY!
WE CAN THROW THE SAME THING BACK AT THEM!
FIRE!
TOOF

YOU...CAN'T... YOU ARE NOT JOR-EL.
HE DIED WITH KRYPTON.
KAL SAID THE SAME THING.
BUT I WAS ABLE TO PERSUADE HIM THAT I AM, INDEED, ALIVE.
YOU... TALKED TO HIM?
WITHIN THE PAST HOUR.
BEFORE HE WAS TAKEN AWAY BY HIS NEVER-ENDING BATTLE AGAINST HUMANITY'S BASE INSTINCTS.
I'M GLAD KELEX SENT ME TO AID YOU, FOR I'VE LONG WANTED TO MEET MY DAUGHTER-IN-LAW.
I'VE WATCHED FROM AFAR AND CAN'T HELP BUT ADMIRE WHAT YOU'VE ADDED TO MY SON'S LIFE.
YOU'VE... WATCHED?
AND HAVEN'T REVEALED YOURSELF UNTIL NOW?
WHY?
THE TIMING HAD TO BE-- WAIT.
HE'S HERE.
FORGIVE THE ABRUPT NATURE OF MY DEPARTURE.
WE'LL MEET AGAIN.
CAN THAT REALLY BE... JOR-EL?
YOU'RE SAFE! THANK GOD!
PLEASE TELL US THAT JON IS HERE!
JIMMY...

"...ARE YOU TELLING ME YOU DON'T **KNOW** WHERE MY SON IS?"
JONATHAN.

I RECOGNIZE THAT VOICE!
YOU'RE THE GUY THAT WAS COACHING ME IN THE FORTRESS!
YES.
THE REASON I WAS ABLE TO ACCESS YOUR FATHER'S FORTRESS AND DO SO...

...IS BECAUSE I AM YOUR **GRAND-FATHER.**
FROM KRYPTON.

WH-WHAT? **HOW?**
DAD SAID HIS PARENTS DIED WHEN KRYPTON BLEW UP.

THAT WAS HIS UNDERSTANDING.
YOUR FATHER WARNS YOU TO BE WARY OF STRANGERS, BUT I HAVE SOMETHING THAT WILL PROVE MY IDENTITY.
LIKE WHAT?

A KRYPTONIAN CRYSTAL. ONE THAT CAN REVEAL YOUR PAST...
...AND **FUTURE.**
FOR **REAL?** THAT'S... **ME?**
IN A FEW YEARS, AT YOUR NEW HOME.

"WE HAVE A LOT TO DISCUSS, JON, BUT NOT HERE.
"WILL YOU COME TO THE FORTRESS WITH ME?"
COMPUTER, EMERGENCY OVERRIDE.
CLICK
OVERRIDE ACCEPTED. WELCOME, MISS JANET.

"DAD LETS YOU GO TO THE FORTRESS?"
A SHAME ABOUT J.B.
BUT THE CHAOS BRINGS US CLOSER TO THE END.

"OF COURSE, JON. WHEN YOU GET DOWN TO THE ESSENCE OF IT ALL...
"...I BUILT THE PLACE."
METROPOLIS WILL DIE...
...SO OZ'S CHOSEN MIGHT LIVE.

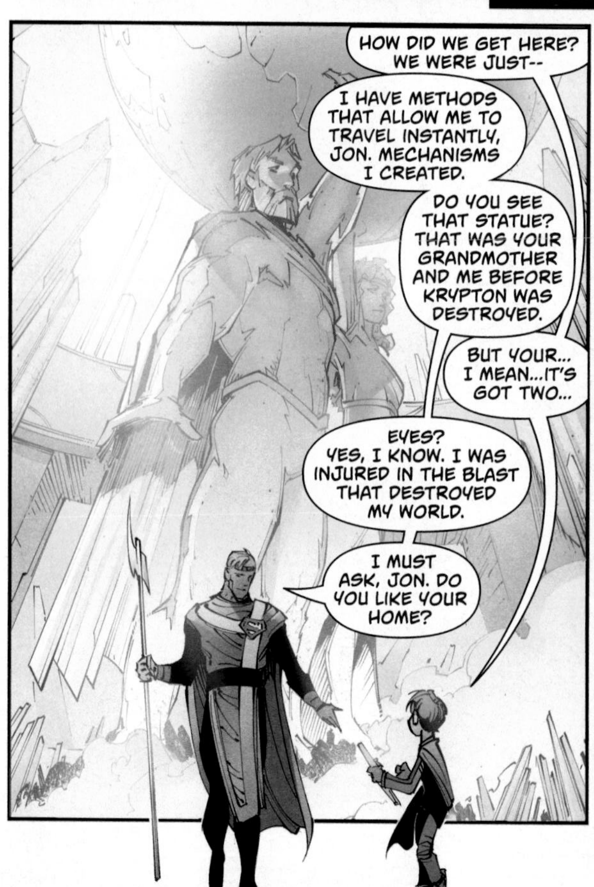
HOW DID WE GET HERE? WE WERE JUST--
I HAVE METHODS THAT ALLOW ME TO TRAVEL INSTANTLY, JON. MECHANISMS I CREATED.
DO YOU SEE THAT STATUE? THAT WAS YOUR GRANDMOTHER AND ME BEFORE KRYPTON WAS DESTROYED.
BUT YOUR... I MEAN...IT'S GOT TWO...
EYES? YES, I KNOW. I WAS INJURED IN THE BLAST THAT DESTROYED MY WORLD.
I MUST ASK, JON. DO YOU LIKE YOUR HOME?

WELL, HAMILTON COUNTY WAS BETTER THAN METROPOLIS.
I AM REFERRING TO EARTH ITSELF, JON. AS LONG AS YOU LIVE HERE...
...YOU'LL HAVE TO HIDE YOUR TRUE NATURE BY WEARING THOSE GLASSES AND THAT SILLY CAP.

YOU'RE LIVING A LIE WHEN YOU DO THAT.
I SUSPECT YOU'D RATHER HAVE FRIENDS YOU CAN OPEN UP TO.
AND NOT SIMPLY THAT BAT-BOY YOU ARE FORCED TO ASSOCIATE WITH.
TALK TO SOMEONE ON YOUR LEVEL ABOUT WHO YOU TRULY ARE, ABILITIES AND ALL.
YEAH...
WHEN I SAVED YOUR FATHER'S LIFE BY SENDING HIM TO EARTH, I THOUGHT HE'D FIND A MORE HOSPITABLE PLACE.
I WAS WRONG.
FORTUNATELY, I HAVE SINCE FOUND A BETTER PLACE.
BETTER THAN EARTH?
MUCH.
IT'S A PLACE WHERE YOU AND YOUR FATHER CAN BE YOURSELVES.
YOU WON'T HAVE TO HIDE BEHIND FAKE NAMES AND DISGUISES. OR ACT AS THOUGH YOU'RE POWERLESS.
HOW CAN THAT BE?
BECAUSE ON THE WORLD I'M SPEAKING OF, NO ONE HAS TO HIDE WHO THEY REALLY ARE.

THIS IS BLISS, JON.
WHERE EVERYONE IS SPECIAL AND NO ONE NEEDS TO HIDE.
THIS IS WHERE YOU SHOULD BE, SON.
THIS IS WHERE ALL OF YOU MUST GO.

EARTH IS ON FIRE.
NO MATTER THE COUNTRY OR PEOPLE...
...MAN HAS DECLARED WAR ON HIS BROTHER.
THE UNTHINKABLE HAS BECOME THE NORM.
INSANITY RULES.

LOGAMBA.
A WORSENING CIVIL WAR HAS BEEN BREWING FOR WEEKS.
IT WENT FULL BORE WHEN THE LOGAMBAN GOVERNMENT FIRED CHEMICAL WEAPONS AT THE REBEL STRONGHOLD.
I PREVENTED THAT FROM BECOMING AN ATROCITY.
THE
BUT THE REBELS RESPONDED BY FIRING THEIR OWN CHEMICAL WEAPONS INTO THE CAPITAL CITY.
THOUSANDS WILL DIE.
UNLESS I CAN STOP IT.
HELP WOULD BE NICE.
BUT FLASH IS HANDLING A MASSIVE RIOT IN PARIS.
DIANA AND ARTHUR ARE DEALING WITH NUCLEAR WASTE DUMPED IN THE PACIFIC.
THE LANTERNS HAVE STOPPED MORE CATASTROPHES TODAY THAN I CAN COUNT.

DAN JURGENS STORY & BREAKDOWN ART
VIKTOR BOGDANOVIC PENCILS
BOGDANOVIC, TREVOR SCOTT
& SCOTT HANNA INKS
MIKE SPICER COLOR • ROB LEIGH LETTERS
NICK BRADSHAW & BRAD ANDERSON COVER
NEIL EDWARDS & JEROMY COX VARIANT COVER
ANDREA SHEA ASSISTANT EDITOR
PAUL KAMINSKI & MIKE COTTON EDITORS
OZ
EFFECT
PART FOUR
SUPERMAN created by JERRY SIEGEL and JOE SHUSTER.
SUPERBOY created by JERRY SIEGEL.
BY SPECIAL ARRANGEMENT WITH THE JERRY SIEGEL FAMILY.
GREEN ARROW AND BLACK CANARY TOOK DOWN A NEO-NAZI ARMS STASH.
SO I'M ON MY OWN.
KARA STOPPED A MASSIVE AMOUNT OF CROPS FROM BEING POISONED.
KONG KENAN DID THE SAME IN CHINA.
WHAT COULD POSSIBLY COMPEL SOMEONE TO POISON FOOD?

LOGAMBA'S ROYAL PALACE.
--CONFIRMED IT WAS NERVE GAS FIRED INTO THE CAPITAL, YOUR EXCELLENCY.
IF NOT FOR THE CAPED AMERICAN, BODIES WOULD LITTER THE STREETS.
MAY I REMIND YOU THAT WE HAVE A FULLY FUNCTIONAL, LIMITED-AREA NUCLEAR DEVICE WE CAN EMPLOY AGAINST THE REBELS?
WE MUST DO SO WHILE THE REBELS ARE STILL FAR FROM THE CITY.
VERY WELL. I WILL NOTIFY...
WAIT. IS THAT--?
WIND?

GYAHH!
NO MORE WASTING TIME.

NOT WHILE PEOPLE ARE DYING.
THESE MEN HAVE TO SETTLE THEIR DIFFERENCES...
...BEFORE IT'S TOO LATE.
WHA--?

YOUR CONFLICT ENDS TODAY.
TALK TO EACH OTHER.
NEGOTIATE.

THE KILLING.
STOPS.
NOW.

THEY WALLOW IN WEALTH WHILE OUR CHILDREN STARVE!
THESE PEOPLE ARE CRUDE AND INFERIOR.
TOO STUPID TO WORK IN OUR INDUSTRIES!

THEN YOU WILL USE YOUR WEALTH TO EDUCATE THEM.
HA!

AND YOU WILL TELL YOUR PEOPLE THAT THEY CAN'T JUST TAKE WHAT THEY WANT.
THEY MUST BE WILLING TO MAKE THE BEST OF THEIR LIVES AND LEARN.
IMPOSSIBLE.

YOU CLAIM TO CARE ABOUT YOUR OWN CHILDREN.
I NEED YOU TO CARE ABOUT EACH OTHER'S.

METROPOLIS.
JON!
WHERE ARE YOU, BUD?
IF HE'S ANYTHING LIKE HIS MOTHER, CURIOSITY GOT THE BETTER OF HIM AND HE'S O
FOLLOWING THE ACTION AROUND HERE.
INSTEAD OF GETTING TO SEE MY OLD JERSEY?
THAT'S HARD TO BELIEVE...
COMICS
IT'S CRAZY OUT THERE, JIMMY. DANGEROUS.
I REALIZE THAT, CHIEF. THAT'S WHY...
"...I GAVE LOIS THE MEANS TO CALL IN THE CAVALRY."
NO LUCK REACHING CLARK AT THE FORTRESS. HE MUST BE KNEE-DEEP IN THE GLOBAL CHAOS.
BUT OUR SON IS MISSING, AND I NEED TO USE ALL THE TOOLS AT MY DISPOSAL.
I NEED SUPERMAN.
ZEEZEE
THE FORTRESS OF SOLITUDE. MOMENTS AGO.
WOW! THIS CITY IS BEAUTIFUL!

WHAT'D YOU CALL IT, AGAIN?
BLISS, JON.
A WONDROUS PLACE WHERE EVERYONE IS BLESSED WITH EXTRAORDINARY ABILITIES.
WHERE EVERYONE IS EQUAL.
EVERYONE CAN LIVE A LIFE TRUE TO HIS OR HER SELF.
I WOULDN'T HAVE TO HIDE WHO I AM?
NEVER.
IF YOU LIVED HERE, YOU'D BE ABLE TO SPEAK OPENLY OF YOUR EMERGING POWERS AND THE JOY OF DISCOVERY.
A SHAME THIS IS JUST A HOLOGRAM OR I'D HAVE YOU INTERACT WITH THEM NOW.
AND YOU KNOW THIS BECAUSE YOU'RE MY GRANDFATHER?
YES, JON. ON KRYPTON, I WAS KNOWN AS JOR-EL, AND I SENT YOUR FATHER TO THIS PLANET EARTH.
I KNOW NOW THAT WAS A MISTAKE.

HIDING ONE'S TRUE NATURE IS AN UNHEALTHY WAY TO LIVE.
WELL, IT SOUNDS GREAT, BUT EARTH IS HOME.
MOM AND DAD'LL NEVER LEAVE.
BESIDES, MOM DOESN'T HAVE POWERS.
SHE WOULDN'T FIT IN AT ALL.
YOUR MOTHER HAS THE BEST POWER OF ALL, JON. HER MIND.
SHE'D DO WELL HERE.
MAYBE. BUT DAD...
HAS TO HIDE BEHIND THAT SILLY KENT IDENTITY, PRETENDING TO BE HUMAN BECAUSE OF HIS ENEMIES.
"CLARK" EXISTS TO PROTECT HIS LOVED ONES. TO PROTECT YOU.
BUT HE DOES GOOD. AND SAVES LOTS OF LIVES!
WHICH IS WONDERFUL. BUT OVER ALL HIS TIME HERE, HAVE HUMANS EVER IMPROVED?
HAVE THESE PEOPLE EVER SHOWN TRUE GRATITUDE, NOT BY SAYING THANK YOU...
...BUT BY ENDING THEIR VIOLENT WAYS?
BY DOING WHAT YOUR FATHER TEACHES?
WELL...
I GUESS NOT.

TO BE CANDID, JON, EVEN IF THEY DID, IT WOULDN'T MATTER.
IT'S TOO LATE.
WHAT? WHY?
THERE'S A THREAT OUT THERE.
A VERY DEADLY AND UNBEATABLE THREAT.
YEAH?
WELL, MY DAD'LL TAKE CARE OF IT!
KRAK
EARTH HAS NEVER SEEN A THREAT LIKE THIS.
IT'S ONE THAT THIS WORLD--AND EVEN YOUR FATHER--CAN'T SURVIVE.
THE JUSTICE LEAGUE--
STANDS NO CHANCE.
THIS ENTIRE PLANE OF EXISTENCE HAS NO FUTURE.
WH-WHAT ARE YOU SAYING--?
THAT'S WHY I'M HERE. TO TAKE YOU ALL TO SAFETY BEFORE--
ZEEZEEE
I'VE KEPT YOU LONG ENOUGH.
IT'S TIME TO GO.

LOGAMBA.
THIS IS NOT WHAT I ENVISIONED...
OR AGREED TO.
EVERY GUN, GRENADE, MACHETE... EVERY WEAPON WE HAD!
FROM BOTH SIDES? IT'S LUNACY!
IF YOU FIGHT NOW, YOU'LL DO SO WITH ROCKS AND STICKS.
ANOTHER REASON TO FIND PEACE.

DON'T--!
BWHOOM
NOW SOLVE THIS.
ZEEZEEE
JIMMY.
HE KNOWS NOT TO USE HIS SIGNAL WATCH UNLESS THERE'S BIG TROUBLE.
HAVE TO ASSUME THE WORST.

THINGS WERE BAD ENOUGH WHEN I LEFT.
SEEM LIKELY THAT THE WORLD CRISES AND OZ'S APPEARANCE ARE CONNECTED SOMEHOW.
METROPOLIS WOULD BE A LOGICAL TARGET--BETTER SCAN THE AREA ON MY WAY TO JIM.
METROPOLIS.
I'M AFRAID I MUST REPORT THAT J.B. IS DEAD. WHICH WAS EXPECTED.
WHAT WE DIDN'T EXPECT IS THAT HE'D FAIL IN HIS MISSION.
THE DAILY PLANET BUILDING STILL STANDS.
NOT ALL OF OUR OPERATIONS CAN BE SUCCESSFUL. FORTUNATELY...
...WE HAVE ARRIVED.
PHASE TWO WILL BE INITIATED.
MR. OZ'S ANOINTED ONES! BLESSED TO HAVE BEEN IN HIS PRESENCE!
AND EMPOWERED TO ACT.
THE EQUIPMENT IS READY. THE TIME HAS COME.
OZ BELIEVES IN OPENNESS AND HONESTY.
THAT THE TRUE NATURE OF MAN MUST BE REVEALED.

HE DEMANDS NOTHING.
ONLY GIVES US THE MEANS TO ACT AS WE DESIRE.
OR GIVE OTHERS THE MEANS TO DO SO.
HE RECOGNIZES THAT MAN IS THE MOST MONSTROUS OF BEASTS
MONSTERS MUST NOT BE ALLOWED TO LIVE.
THIS GAS WILL PURGE THE CITY OF LIFE.
THIS IS WHERE METROPOLIS DIES...
...WHILE WE, THE DESERVING, LIVE ON TO SHAPE THE WORLD AS WE SEE FIT.
OH...
KRUNG
WE WILL TRUST OZ TO COME.
TO SAVE US.

BRA-
...YOU WILL GET WHAT YOU DESERVE.
KA-KRASH

WAIT A MINUTE-- YOU'RE DRESSED LIKE THE MEN WHO TRIED TO CAPTURE DOOMSDAY!
AN OFFERING TO THE DIVINE MR. OZ!
OZ?
YOU WORK FO JOR-EL?
WE SERVE OZ!
WE PUT HUMAN SOCIETY IN POSITION TO REVEAL ITS TRUE NATURE!
AND HUMANS ALWAYS--
--FAIL!
CHOOM
SO THERE IT IS. NO MATTER IF OZ REALLY IS MY FATHER OR NOT--
--HE IS INVOLVED IN ALL THIS MADNESS.
KZZT
BUT WHY?!

SO I SEE HOW **BAD** PEOPLE CAN BE?
THE EVIL **MUST** BE WIPED AWAY!
THE **GAS!**

WHATEVER EVIL YOU THINK YOU'RE ATTACKING...
...YOU'RE JUST AS BAD.

NOTHING WILL PASS THROUGH THOSE PIPES.
NOTHING.
YOU'RE RUINING **EVERYTHING!**
DON'T YOU UNDERSTAND?!
OZ WON'T SAVE YOU.
HE'S TRYING TO MAKE A POINT...
...AND USING **YOU** TO DO IT.

WORLD'S TURMOIL-- COORDINATED.
AND IT'S OZ PULLING THE STRINGS.
ZEEZEEE
JIMMY'S ALARM.
I PRAY I
TOO

LOIS?!
I EXPECTED--
JIMMY LOANED ME HIS WATCH.
JON IS MISSING!
I THINK IT'S CONNECTED TO THIS MAN WHO APPEARED-- WHO CLAIMED TO BE--
JOR-EL.
HE SAVED ME FROM A BOMBER.
IN THE EXCITEMENT, JON DISAPPEARED!
HE CAN'T REALLY BE JOR-EL, CAN HE?
MAYBE... I'M NOT SURE.
EVERYTHING THAT'S HAPPENING... THE PEOPLE WITH OZ TATTOOS...
I THINK HE'S BEHIND IT ALL.
ONLY TO THE EXTENT THAT I ALLOW THE PEOPLE OF THIS WORLD TO PROVE HOW GHASTLY THEY REALLY ARE.

I KNOW THE TRUTH ABOUT HUMANITY, KAL.
NOW YOU DO AS WELL.
IF YOU ACCEPT THAT, YOU COULDN'T POSSIBLY WANT TO RAISE JON IN THIS CESSPOOL.
STEP AWAY FROM MY SON.
YOU HAD NO RIGHT TO TAKE HIM.
HE DIDN'T TAKE ME, DAD!
I WENT WITH HIM.
WILLINGLY!
HE'S BEEN HELPING ME--EVEN BACK WHEN WE WERE FIGHTING ZOD IN THE FORTRESS!
HE WANTS WHAT'S BEST FOR US!

JON SPEAKS THE TRUTH, KAL.
I HAVE DEDICATED MY LIFE TO DOING WHAT'S RIGHT.
FIRST, BY TRYING TO SAVE KRYPTON.
THOUGH I FAILED...
...I KNEW YOU WOULD HAVE THE OPPORTUNITY TO DO THE SAME HERE.
YOUR SURVIVAL HAS ALWAYS BEEN EVERYTHING TO ME.
IT'S WHY I TOOK POSSESSION OF DOOMSDAY.
WHY I LOCKED UP MXYZPTLK AND ENDED THE THREAT OF METALLO.
WHAT... ARE YOU SAYING?
YOU ARE FINALLY BEGINNING TO APPRECIATE PEOPLE FOR WHAT THEY REALLY ARE.
AN UNDESERVING MASS OF SELFISHNESS, GREED AND VIOLENCE.
JUDGMENT DAY IS COMING, SON.

A THREAT SO MASSIVE THAT EARTH--AND YOU--HAVE NO CHANCE OF SURVIVING.
I SAVED YOU ONCE AND WILL DO SO AGAIN.
YOU AND YOUR FAMILY.
YOU MUST LEAVE NOW...
...OR YOU WILL PERISH.
THIS... INSANITY CAN'T CONTINUE.
I DON'T KNOW WHO YOU REALLY ARE, BUT YOU CAN'T POSSIBLY BE MY FATHER.
AND IF, SOMEHOW, YOU ARE...
...YOU AREN'T THE HERO I BELIEVED YOU TO BE.
STEP ASIDE, JON.
NO, DAD!
NO!

YOU GOTTA LISTEN TO GRANDDAD!
IF WE DON'T GO--
--WE'RE ALL GONNA
DIE!

I NEVER KNEW MY FATHER.
I WAS A BABY WHEN HE PUT ME IN A ROCKET AND SENT ME FAR AWAY FROM THE DOOMED PLANET OF KRYPTON.
HE DIED. MY WORLD DIED.
THIS MAN BEFORE ME...THIS MR. OZ... CLAIMS TO BE THAT VERY SAME FATHER WHO SAVED ME ALL THOSE YEARS AGO.
THE OZ EFFECT
CONCLUSION
IS HE A FRAUD? A LIAR?
OR IS HE TELLING THE TRUTH?
YOU GOTTA LISTEN TO GRANDDAD!
HE SAYS WE HAVE TO LEAVE EARTH. EVERYONE ON IT IS GONNA DIE!
WHAT MATTERS NOW IS THAT MY SON BELIEVES HIM...
...WHICH MEANS I HAVE TO GET THIS MAN THE HELL AWAY FROM JON.
DAN JURGENS STORY & BREAKDOWN ART
VIKTOR BOGDANOVIC PENCILS
BOGDANOVIC, TREVOR SCOTT & SCOTT HANNA INKS
MIKE SPICER COLOR • ROB LEIGH LETTERS
NICK BRADSHAW & BRAD ANDERSON COVER
YANICK PAQUETTE & NATHAN FAIRBAIRN VARIANT COVER
ANDREA SHEA ASSISTANT EDITOR
PAUL KAMINSKI & MIKE COTTON EDITORS
EDDIE BERGANZA GROUP EDITOR
SUPERMAN created by JERRY SIEGEL and JOE SHUSTER.
SUPERBOY created by JERRY SIEGEL.
BY SPECIAL ARRANGEMENT WITH THE JERRY SIEGEL FAMILY.

YOU CALLED HIM... GRANDDAD?
INDEED, HE DID.
MY GRANDSON IS AN INTELLIGENT YOUNG MAN.
YOU HAVE NO RIGHT TO TALK TO--
BUT IT'S TRUE, DAD!
HE'S JOR-EL!
CLARK.
IF THERE'S ANY CHANCE IT'S TRUE, YOU CAN'T ATTACK YOUR FATHER.
IT'S MORE THAN THAT, LOIS...
FOR MONTHS NOW WE'VE BEEN WARNED THAT SOMEONE WAS OUT THERE... SOMEONE DANGEROUS...
...AND IT'S TRUE. I'VE SEEN THE PROOF.
MR. OZ IS RESPONSIBLE FOR THE WORLD'S CHAOS...
...AND THIS MAN IS OZ!
WHY... WOULD HE DO THAT?
DAD, GIVE HIM A CHANCE...

...AND LISTEN TO HIM!
HE SAYS EARTH IS DOOMED!
THE ONLY THREAT HERE IS HIM.
I AM NOT RESPONSIBLE FOR TODAY'S ATROCITIES OR THE NIGHTMARE TO COME, KAL.
I DON'T BELIEVE YOU.
I CAN'T BELIEVE A SINGLE WORD YOU'VE SAID.
I POSITIONED PEOPLE IN SITUATIONS WHERE THEY WERE GIVEN A CHOICE BETWEEN GOOD AND EVIL.
EVIL WON.
WHICH IS WHY EARTH'S FATE IS SEALED.
I DID THIS SO YOU WOULD SEE...
...AND ACCEPT THESE PEOPLE FOR THE IRREDEEMABLE BEINGS THEY ARE.
RAKK
FSASH
I WASN'T SAVED FROM KRYPTON'S DESTRUCTION BECAUSE OF ANYTHING I'VE DONE. THIS ISN'T ABOUT ME.
I WAS SAVED...

...BECAUSE THIS IS ABOUT *YOU.*
WHERE--?
AT FIRST, IT WAS MY PRISON.
NOW MY HOME. FREE FROM THE RESTRAINTS OF TIME AND SPACE.

WHEN EARTH DIES...
...LIKE SO MANY DOOMED WORLDS BEFORE IT...
...THIS PLACE WILL PROVIDE SAFE HAVEN.

IF A THREAT OF THAT MAGNITUDE LOOMS OVER EARTH, I WON'T BE *HERE.*
I'LL BE *THERE.*
FIGHTING TO SAVE IT.

DO SO, AND YOU WILL DIE.
AS WILL YOUR WIF AND CHIL
I'VE HAD *ENOUGH* OF YOUR REFUSAL TO ACCEPT THE *TRUTH.*

AND IF YOU WON'T ACT TO SAVE YOURSELF AND YOUR FAMILY...
...I WILL.
SHRAK

BAD GUYS ALWAYS HAVE SOME DEMENTED EXPLANATION FOR WHY THEY DO WRONG.
MOST TIMES, THEY'RE HOLLOW EXCUSES.
NONE OF THEM REALLY BELIEVE WHAT THEY'RE SAYING.
SKOOM
THIS IS DIFFERENT.

HE SEEMS CERTAIN OF ALL THIS.
CAN'T YOU ACCEPT THAT I'M TRYING TO HELP YOU, KAL?
SHAKK
EARTH.
IS.
SICK.
YOU NEEDED TO SEE THAT FOR YOURSELF, AND MR. OZ WAS THE VEHICLE THAT ALLOWED IT TO HAPPEN.
MAN HIMSELF HAS PROVEN THAT HIS FUTURE IS HOPELESS.
IF YOU KNEW ANYTHING ABOUT ME...
...UNDERSTOOD ANYTHING ABOUT WHAT AND WHO I AM...
IF YOU'RE REALLY WHOM YOU CLAIM YOU ARE...
...WHY THE CHARADE? WHY MASQUERADE AS MR. OZ?
WHY NOT SIMPLY TALK TO ME? LET ME HELP YOU?
THOOM
...YOU NEVER WOULD HAVE LET THAT VIOLENCE HAPPEN!

THAT FELT LIKE PUNCHING A KRYPTONIAN.
BRAM
COULD HE REALLY BE...?
WHAT SON...
...STRIKES HIS FATHER?
HOW COULD MY FATHER...
...LET INNOCENT PEOPLE DIE?
KRAKKK
THIS ROOM...
MXYZPTLK TALKED ABOUT BEING LOCKED UP...WONDERED WHY I NEVER SAVED HIM!*
YOU WERE HIS JAILER?
I'VE BEEN SAYING IT ALL ALONG, KAL.
I'M HERE TO SAVE YOU.

YET YOU DON'T APPRECIATE IT!
SKAZZ
K-- KRYPTONITE?
HOW--?

RATHER THAN LET IT KILL ME, AS IT SHOULD HAVE...
...I'VE BEEN EVOLVED TO CONTROL IT.

NNGH!
HURTS...
...HAVE TO FIGHT BACK...
...WHILE I STILL CAN.
KRAMM
PRESS THE ATTACK...
...BEFORE...
MY GOD.

DOOMSDAY?!
BUT... I SENT HIM TO THE PHANTOM ZONE.
I'M THE ONE WHO DISCOVERED THE PHANTOM ZONE.
INTERCEPTING THE PROJECTOR'S BEAM TO BRING HIM HERE WAS SIMPLICITY ITSELF.
I CEDED CONTROL OF DANGEROUS FORCES IN THE PAST, KAL.
NEVER AGAIN.
NOW AND ALWAYS, I WILL MAINTAIN AN IRON GRIP ON MY FAMILY'S DESTINY.

I FEARED SOMEONE WOULD FIND DOOMSDAY... USE HIM AGAINST YOU.
HE IS YOUR MOST LETHAL ENEMY...
...AND YOU'LL NOT ESCAPE DEATH A SECOND TIME.
YOU'RE... PROTECTING ME.
AS I KEEP SAYING, THAT HAS BEEN MY ONLY OBJECTIVE, KAL.
FROM THE MOMENT YOU TOOK YOUR FIRST BREATH TO THE MOMENT I PUT YOU IN THAT ROCKET...
...UNTIL NOW...
...I'VE TRIED TO HELP.
THIS IS FOR YOUR OWN DAMN GOOD.
SKAZZ
GYAHH!

CHAKK

I DON'T LIKE DOING THIS, BUT I KNOW WHAT'S COMING, KAL.
IT'S SO MUCH BIGGER--SO MUCH MORE POWERFUL THAN YOU.
I CAN SAVE YOU...
...IF YOU LET ME.

BUT WHO'S GOING TO SAVE ME FROM YOU?

KRYPTONITE...
...THE SINGLE MOST LETHAL WEAPON IN EXISTENCE...
...IS YOURS TO COMMAND...

...YET YOU USE IT AGAINST YOUR OWN FLESH AND BLOOD?

YOUR OWN SON?!
SNAPPT
Uh...
UH...
YAHHHH!
SSSSSS
THE ENERGY SURROUNDING THIS STAFF IS TOXIC.
I FELT IT FROM THE MOMENT I MET YOU. BUT THE REAL QUESTION IS...WERE YOU CONTROLLING IT...
...OR WAS IT CONTROLLING YOU?
Y--YOU DON'T UNDERSTAND...
...THE KRYPTONITE--!

THE KRYPTONITE?
WHAT ARE YOU SAYING?
AFTER... THE EXPLOSION...
...LODGED... IN MY SKULL...
...THE STAFF... RELIEVED THE PAIN... AND MORE...
...BUT IT MADE ME... HE MADE ME...
I--
I NEVER MEANT TO HURT ANYONE.
I NEVER KNEW MY FATHER.
HE DIED SAVING ME FROM A DOOMED WORLD.
I-- I'M SICK, SON.
I DIDN'T--
WE HAVE TO FIND HELP FOR YOU.
IT WAS A TRAGEDY HE TRIED TO PREVENT, BUT HIS OWN PEOPLE WOULDN'T LET HIM.
WOULDN'T LISTEN.
MAYBE THERE'S SOMETHING IN THE FORTRESS...THE RECOVERY SUIT...SOMETHING WE CAN USE.
STAY BACK, KAL.
OR YOU'LL BE AFFECTED, TOO.
THIS SICKNESS. WHAT IT DID TO ME...EVERYTHING I EXPERIENCED...
I'M THE ONE WHO'S SORRY, KAL.
PEOPLE LET MY FATHER DOWN. THEY LET THEMSELVES DOWN.
AND MY FATHER WAS THE ONLY ONE WHO COULD SEE IT.
I KNOW THE IDEALS YOU REPRESENT.
WHAT YOU MEAN TO YOUR WORLD.

I WON'T LET YOU DIE...
...FATHER.
NO!
HE'S COMING!
I CAN FEEL IT!
FIND LOIS AND JON, SON!
FIGHT FOR THEM.
SAVE THEM.
DAD?!

HE'S TAKING ME!
JUST REMEMBER...
...THAT I LOVE YOU, KAL.
I ALWAYS HAVE.
AND ALWAYS WILL.
YOU CAN'T HAVE HIM!
I WON'T LET YOU TAKE MY FATH--
PASSH
--ER.

WHAT DO YOU WANT FROM ME?
WHO ARE YOU?!
NGH!
CAN'T--!
CAN'T...

THE FORTRESS.
IF THE BEING THAT'S OUT THERE CAN SEND ME BACK HERE SO EASILY...

...HE'S AS POWERFUL AND DANGEROUS AS JOR-EL SAYS.
HE TOOK MY FATHER FROM THE BRINK OF DEATH.
BROKE HIM.

TWISTED HIM.
SOMEHOW MADE IT SEEM RIGHT...

...TO SHOW ME MAN AT HIS WORST.
BUT WHAT IF HE'S RIGHT?

ARE WE AS LOST AS HE SAYS?
WE SHOULD GET INSIDE, JON.
WHO KNOWS WHEN THEY'LL BE BACK?
MOM, LOOK!

YOU'RE ALONE?
WHERE IS HE?
WHERE'S GRANDDAD?
I'M SORRY, JON. I COULDN'T STOP IT.
HE...WAS TAKEN.
BUT... YOU SAVE PEOPLE!
WHY COULDN'T YOU SAVE HIM?
HE'S SOMEWHERE OUT THERE, JON.
I'LL FIND HIM.
I PROMISE.
YOU'RE SAYING THAT MAN REALLY IS YOUR FATHER?
I'M SAYING HE'S A SICK MAN, WARPED BY HIS PAST, WHO WANTED ME TO SEE THE WORLD AT ITS WORST.
IF I ARRIVED HERE AND HAD AN EXPERIENCE LIKE HIS, WOULD I SEE THINGS THE SAME WAY?
WOULD I THINK EARTH IS A WORLD WITHOUT HOPE?
BUT WHAT ABOUT THE REST?
ABOUT EARTH BEING DOOMED?
FROM AN OUTSIDE THREAT...
...AS WELL AS ITS OWN PEOPLE?

...AMOUNT OF BLOOD DESCRIBED AS...
...VICTIMIZED...
...CHILD...
...SOCIAL WORKER FOUND DEAD...
...CLINIC FIREBOMBED...
...OPPRESSED...
...ASSAULT WEAPONS...
...POOR...
...SCAM...
...LIFELESS...
...OPPRESSED...
...DIRECTIONLESS TEENS...
...HATE CRIME...
...SCAM...
...BEATEN...
...HOB'S BAY SHOOTING VICTIM...
...DISDAIN...
...HATE SPEECH...
...ASSAULT...
...CHILD...
...INCREASING NEED FOR FOOD STAMPS...
LOOTERS ONCE AGAIN TORE APART HOMES IN THE FLOOD-RAVAGED CITY...
...SIMPLE DRONE WITH A GRENADE...
...YET ANOTHER GOVERNMENT OFFICIAL INDICTED...
...LAUGHED AS HE STABBED...
...VICTIMS LEFT WITH NOTHING...
...POLICE OFFICERS AMBUSHED IN THEIR SQUAD CARS WHILE RESPONDING TO A CALL...
...UNRESTRAINED GRAFT AND CORRUPTION...
...SCAM...
...LAST SEEN ALIVE...
...IGNORED THE CRIES FOR HELP...
...PARTY TURNED VIOLENT...
...MOST BRAZEN TERRORIST ATTACK EVER...
...SOLDIERS DEFENDING A VILLAGE FROM LOCAL MILITANTS...
...HOPEFUL IMMIGRANTS SUFFOCATED IN A SWELTERING TRUCK WHEN IT WAS ABANDONED...
...ON THE VERGE OF PERFECTING A NUCLEAR WEAPON...
...DESTROYED BY AN ARSONIST...
...JOBLESS RATES RISING...
...BEDRIDDEN NURSING HOME PATIENTS DIED FROM NEGLECT WHEN...
...BURNING CROSS FOUND ON A FAMILY'S LAWN...
...SUICIDE RATE AMONG VETERANS...
...SWINDLED AN ELDERLY COUPLE OUT OF THEIR LIFE SAVINGS...
...DISCOVERED THE REMAINS...
...LOVE IT OR LEAVE IT...
IN A MIDDLE SCHOOL LOCKER...
...WHERE POLICE HAVE REPORTEDLY SHOT AN UNARMED MAN...
...DIDN'T NOTICE THE MAN'S BODY AS THEY WALKED PAST...
...LACK OF FAITH...
...UNITED NATIONS RELIEF TEAM ATTACKED...
...RAMPANT POVERTY...
...TAKEN FROM A SCHOOL PLAYGROUND...
...SOUTHERN CHURCH FIREBOMBED...
...ELECTION INTERFERENCE...
...WIDENING EDUCATION GAP...
...DECLINE IN THE STANDARD OF LIVING...
...RACIAL CONFLICT BOILED OVER...
...LOCAL MOSQUE WAS THE SUBJECT OF VANDALISM WHEN...
...PERSONAL INFORMATION HACKED AND RELEASED...
...INCREASING RATE OF VIOLENCE...
...LIMITING FREEDOM OF SPEECH...
...RAMPANT GANG ACTIVITY TERRORIZING THE NEIGHBORHOOD...
...DENIED MEDICAL CARE...
...ROUND OF LAYOFFS...
...ASSAULT WEAPONS...
...FORCED HIS WAY IN...
...PRISON RIOT...
...UNRESTRAINED CHAOS...
...DIRECTIONLESS TEENS...
...BEATEN AND ROBBED...
...SOCIAL WORKER FOUND DEAD...
...ROBBERY...
...CHEMICAL WEAPONS TO BE USED IN AN ATTACK...
...AMOUNT OF BLOOD DESCRIBED AS...

...SITUATION DESCRIBED AS BEYOND HOPE.
CLARK?
ARE YOU OKAY?

PEOPLE ARE LOSING HOPE, LOIS.

WHERE ARE YOU GOING, DAD?
BACK TO WORK.

I NEVER KNEW MY BIOLOGICAL FATHER...
...AT LEAST NOT THE WAY MOST PEOPLE DO.
ALL MY LIFE I HEARD HIS RECORDED VOICE, SAW IMAGES OF WHAT HE LOOKED LIKE...
...BUT I NEVER KNEW WHO HE WAS. NOT REALLY.
I HAD TO BELIEVE IN MY HEART THAT HE WAS A GOOD MAN.
COMPUTER, BEGIN REBOOT OF PROGRAM. DESIGNATE: KELEX.
INITIALIZING.
COMPILE ALL FILES PERTAINING TO JOR-EL AND CROSS-REFERENCE WITH KEYWORD "MR. OZ."
HE HAS TO BE A GOOD MAN. BECAUSE IF HE'S NOT...

...THEN WHAT DOES THAT MAKE ME?
SYSTEM CHECK COMPLETE. I AM UNCOMPROMISED.
HI-FI color
ROB LEIGH letters
FRANCIS MANAPUL cover
JERRY ORDWAY & HI-FI variant cover
ANDREA SHEA assistant editor
PAUL KAMINSKI editor
EDDIE BERGANZA group editor
SUPERMAN created by Jerry Siegel and Joe Shuster. SUPERBOY created by Jerry Siegel.
By special arrangement with the Jerry Siegel family.

DAN JURGENS story • ROB WILLIAMS script • WILL CONRAD art
AFTEREFFECTS
HELLO, KAL-EL.
HOW MAY I SERVE YOU?
KELEX. CHECK YOUR PROGRAMMING PARAMETERS. FULL SYSTEM SCAN. INFORM ME OF ANY VIRUSES OR RECENT ALTERATIONS. ARE YOU COMPROMISED IN ANY WAY?
WHO IS YOUR MASTER?
WHO DO YOU ANSWER TO?
JOR-EL.
...
WHO IS MR. OZ?
JOR-EL.

NO!
THIS HOUSE WAS MEANT TO BE A FORTRESS.
A PLACE THAT WAS MINE ALONE...
...BUT HE'S IN HERE, ISN'T HE?
HE ALWAYS WAS.
MR. OZ DID AWFUL THINGS... MANIPULATED PEOPLE...
...I REFUSE TO ACCEPT THAT HE'S JOR-EL. I CAN'T! I...
I...
...
...I DON'T KNOW WHO I AM.
YOU BROKE YOUR LITTLE TABLE.

BRUCE?
I DIDN'T HEAR THE BATPLANE APPROACHING.
NO...
...YOU DIDN'T.
LOOKS LIKE YOU WERE BUSY.
YOU CAN'T DO THIS, CLARK. YOU LOSING YOUR TEMPER, GETTING RECKLESS. IT'S NOT THE SAME FOR THE REST OF US. IT'S...

DANGEROUS?
IS THAT WHY YOU'RE HERE, BRUCE? TO MAKE SURE THE POWERFUL ALIEN IS IN CHECK?

ARE YOU WORRIED ABOUT WHAT I'M CAPABLE OF?
NO.

I CAME BECAUSE I WAS CONCERNED ABOUT YOU.
YOU'VE BEEN AT THIS FOR SOME TIME.
...
YOU DON'T KNOW WHAT THIS IS LIKE, BRUCE. YOU THINK YOU KNOW YOUR PLACE IN THE UNIVERSE, AND THEN YOU REALIZE...
...YOU DON'T KNOW ANYTHING.
WHAT WOULD YOU DO IF YOUR FATHER JUST SHOWED UP IN YOUR LIFE AGAIN? THE FATHER YOU THOUGHT WAS DEAD.
THAT'S PART OF WHY I'M HERE.
I DO KNOW WHAT YOU'RE GOING THROUGH. I FACED SOMETHING SIMILAR MYSELF RECENTLY.*
*SEE BATMAN/FLASH "THE BUTTON." --Paul again
SOME LIFE, huh?
Hrm.
THIS ISN'T JUST YOU, CLARK.
SOMETHING IS WRONG WITH TIME.

CLARK?
TROUBLE. I'M PICKING UP SOMETHING.
ANYTHING I CAN--
NO. THANK YOU.
THEY NEED ME NOW.
YOU'RE SUPERMAN.
DON'T FORGET IT.
FOR A SECOND, I THINK IT'S A RELIEF TO HAVE A CRISIS TO FACE.
IT FEELS GOOD TO HAVE THE CHANCE TO BE HEROIC.
AND THEN FEELING GOOD GOES AWAY...
"KENT!"

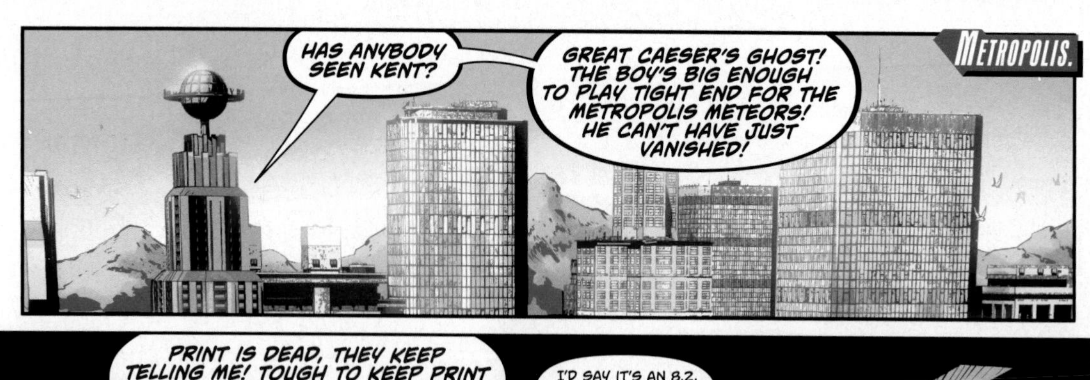
METROPOLIS.
HAS ANYBODY SEEN KENT?
GREAT CAESER'S GHOST! THE BOY'S BIG ENOUGH TO PLAY TIGHT END FOR THE METROPOLIS METEORS! HE CAN'T HAVE JUST VANISHED!

PRINT IS DEAD, THEY KEEP TELLING ME! TOUGH TO KEEP PRINT ALIVE IF AN EDITOR CAN'T FIND HIS DAMN REPORTERS FOR DAYS ON END!
I'D SAY IT'S AN 8.2, LOIS. IF YOU KNOW WHERE CLARK IS, I'D GET WORD TO...
I GOT THIS, JIMMY.

CLARK'S ON A STORY, PERRY. DEEP COVER.
WHAT? HE'S BEEN GONE FOR DAYS. WHY DIDN'T HE TELL ME?
NO TIME. HE HAD TO GO RIGHT AWAY OR LOSE THE SOURCE.

YEAH? WHAT'S THE STORY? HE WAS WORKING ON THE DOCKSIDE DEVELOPMENT.
CORRUPTION CLAIMS AGAINST SENATOR McVAY.
I THOUGHT THAT WAS YOUR STORY?
WE'RE MARRIED, PERRY. WE'VE BEEN WORKING IT TOGETHER. THIS IS A BIG LEAD.
COVERING FOR YOUR HUSBAND, LOIS?

SOMETIMES YOU HAVE TO FOLLOW YOUR INSTINCTS. YOU KNOW THAT. EVEN IF THEY SEEM EXTREME.
SO, I GUESS THIS COMES DOWN TO ONE POINT, PERRY...
...DO YOU TRUST YOUR REPORTERS, OR DON'T YOU?

TELL KENT TO CALL ME THE MOMENT YOU HEAR FROM HIM.

I WOULDN'T WANT TO **COMPROMISE** HIM.

DAMMIT, CLARK.
WHERE **ARE** YOU?
"SOMETIMES YOU HAVE TO FOLLOW YOUR INSTINCTS. EVEN IF THEY SEEM EXTREME."
THAT'S SOME GOOD ADVICE, MISS LANE.

WHERE HAVE YOU BEEN?
I'VE BEEN WORRIED ABOUT YOU.
JON HAS BEEN WORRIED ABOUT YOU.
TRYING TO FIND ANSWERS. FAILING...
I THOUGHT I COULD HELP PEOPLE. THAT IT WOULD GET MY MIND OFF THIS MR. OZ BUSINESS. BUT...
...THERE WERE 250 TERRIFIED REFUGEES ON ONE SINKING BOAT, LOIS. ONE SMALL BOAT.
CHILDREN...FAMILIES. RUNNING FROM SOMETHING WORSE THAN DROWNING.
HOW MANY BOATS DON'T I GET TO?
...
WHAT IF MR. OZ WAS RIGHT ABOUT HUMANITY?
WHAT IF WE ARE BEYOND SAVING?
HE'S NOT RIGHT.
YOU'LL SHOW HIM.
SUPERMAN.
HAL?
THE CORPS HAS THE FILE YOU REQUESTED.
IT'S ON MOGO. I'M CREATING AN OPENING IN TRANSLUMINAL SPACE FOR YOU NOW AT YOUR POSITION.

I... I'M...
DON'T BE. I UNDERSTAND.
YOU HAVE TO KNOW.
"GO."

CURRENT HEADQUARTERS OF THE GREEN LANTERN COR
SUPERMAN.
IT'S GOOD TO SEE YOU.
I JUST WISH IT WAS UNDER HAPPIER CIRCUMSTANCES.
SO DO I, HAL.
THANK YOU FOR THIS. I APPRECIATE IT.
YOU'RE ALWAYS WELCOME HERE. YOU KNOW THAT.

I'M SURE THE FILES OF TOMAR-RE WILL GIVE YOU ANSWERS.
HE WAS THE LANTERN IN CHARGE OF SECTOR 2813.
IS THERE ANYTHING IN PARTICULAR YOU NEED TO...
KRYPTON.
I NEED TO SEE THE MOMENT KRYPTON EXPLODED.
I NEED TO KNOW THAT ONLY ONE SHIP ESCAPED.
SALAAK, CAN YOU...?
I HAVE IT, JORDAN. BRINGING IT...
...UP.
SUPERMAN. THIS ISN'T A SIMULATION. IT'S A RECORDING.
THIS IS ACTUALLY KRYPTON AS IT APPEARED JUST PRIOR TO ITS DESTRUCTION.

THAT...
...THAT'S ME...IT'S MY ROCKET.
TOMAR-RE'S RECORDING OF THE SECTOR HAS THIS LAUNCH AT SECONDS BEFORE THE--
FZZT
THERE'S SOMETHING WRONG WITH THE FILE!
IT'S JAMMED. DISTORTED. THIS...IT ISN'T RIGHT.
I'LL MOVE THE FOOTAGE FORWARD A CLICK...
WHAT?
THAT'S... STRANGE.

NO.
THE MOMENT OF KRYPTON'S DESTRUCTION HAS BEEN...CORRUPTED ON OUR FILES.
THIS IS *VERY* UNUSUAL.
IF I DIDN'T KNOW BETTER I'D SAY IT HAS BEEN TAMPERED WITH.
IT'S NOT JUST THE FILE.
SOMETHING TAMPERED WITH *TIME*.
SOME*ONE* HAS DONE THIS.

METROPOLIS.
YOU'RE BACK.
I DIDN'T WANT TO WAKE JON.
DID YOU FIND IT? WHAT YOU WERE LOOKING FOR.
NO.
SOMETHING'S VERY WRONG, LOIS.
AND THIS ISN'T JUST ABOUT ME. IF WHATEVER'S OUT THERE CAN DO THIS, IF HE CAN ALTER TIME ITSELF...
...HOW CAN I FIGHT THAT?

YOU'LL FIND A WAY.
YOU ALWAYS DO.
THIS... THIS IS ABOUT FINDING OUT WHO I AM.
IF I'M HIS SON, WHAT DOES THAT SAY ABOUT ME? WHAT DOES IT SAY ABOUT JON...?
YOU'RE THE BEST FATHER JON COULD EVER DREAM OF.
AND MORE THAN THAT, CLARK...
...YOU'RE A REPORTER. THE SECOND-BEST ONE AT THE DAILY PLANET, IN FACT.
WHATEVER YOU'RE LOOKING FOR...

"...YOU'LL TRACK IT DOWN."
JUSTICE LEAGUE WATCHTOWER.
"SOMETIMES YOU HAVE TO FOLLOW YOUR INSTINCTS. YOU KNOW THAT...
"...EVEN IF THEY SEEM EXTREME."
MY WIFE IS A VERY SMART WOMAN.
FLASH'S COSMIC TREADMILL.
HIS OWN PERSONAL TIME MACHINE.
HE ONCE SHOWED ME HOW TO SET THE TIME AND LOCATION.
IF FLASH CAN GO BACK IN TIME...

...LET'S SEE IF I CAN DO THE SAME.
I NEED TO SEE...
...Nnnnn...
...FOR MYSELF.
I NEED TO KNOW THE TRUTH!
I HAVE TO GO BACK TO KRYPTON!
WAIT!

SUPERMAN!
DON'T!
IT APPEARS, BOOSTER, WE HAVE ARRIVED A SECOND TOO LATE AND SUPERMAN HAS ALREADY LEFT FOR THE PAST VIA THE TIME STREAM.
NOW THE TIMELINE ITSELF IS IN DANGER OF TOTAL COLLAPSE!
OOPS.

THE OZ EFFECT
VARIANT COVER GALLERY

ACTION COMICS #985 variant cover by NEIL EDWARDS and JEROMY COX

ACTION COMICS #986 variant cover by NEIL EDWARDS and JEROMY COX

ACTION COMICS #987 variant cover by NEIL EDWARDS and JEROMY COX

ACTION COMICS #988 variant cover by NEIL EDWARDS and JEROMY COX

ACTION COMICS #989 variant cover by NEIL EDWARDS and JEROMY COX

ACTION COMICS #990 variant cover by NEIL EDWARDS and JEROMY COX

ACTION COMICS #991 variant cover by YANICK PAQUETTE and NATHAN FAIRBAIRN

ACTION COMICS #992 variant cover by JERRY ORDWAY and HI-FI

MR. OZ CHARACTER SKETCHES BY
JORGE JIMENEZ

UNUSED COVERS BY
NICK BRADSHAW

Unused cover art for ACTION COMICS #987
with color by JASON WRIGHT

Unused cover art for ACTION COMICS #988
with color by BRAD ANDERSON

EARLY ISSUE BREAKDOWN FEATURING COVER SKETCHES BY **JIM LEE**

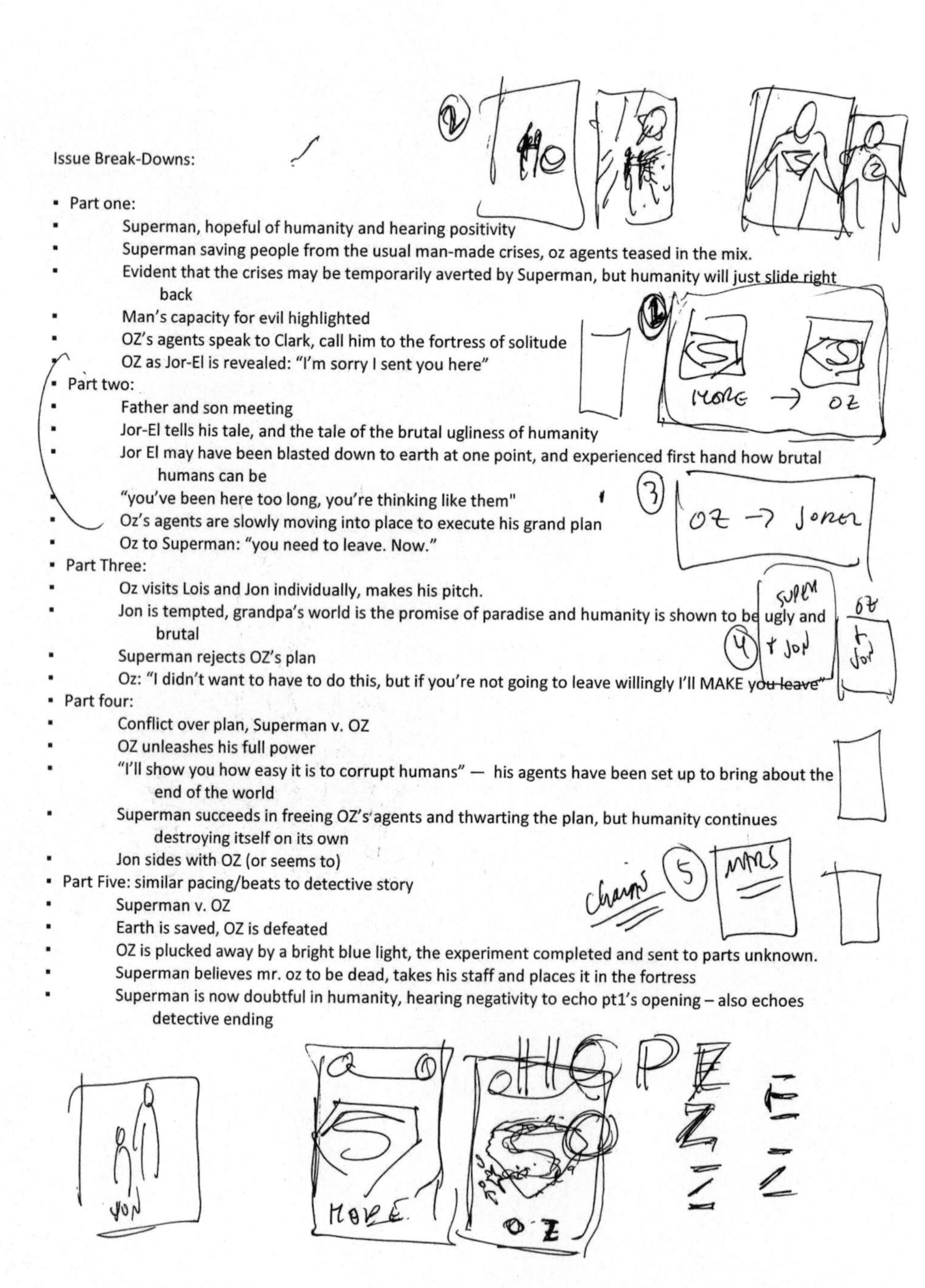

Issue Break-Downs:

- Part one:
- Superman, hopeful of humanity and hearing positivity
- Superman saving people from the usual man-made crises, oz agents teased in the mix.
- Evident that the crises may be temporarily averted by Superman, but humanity will just slide right back
- Man's capacity for evil highlighted
- OZ's agents speak to Clark, call him to the fortress of solitude
- OZ as Jor-El is revealed: "I'm sorry I sent you here"
- Part two:
- Father and son meeting
- Jor-El tells his tale, and the tale of the brutal ugliness of humanity
- Jor El may have been blasted down to earth at one point, and experienced first hand how brutal humans can be
- "you've been here too long, you're thinking like them"
- Oz's agents are slowly moving into place to execute his grand plan
- Oz to Superman: "you need to leave. Now."
- Part Three:
- Oz visits Lois and Jon individually, makes his pitch.
- Jon is tempted, grandpa's world is the promise of paradise and humanity is shown to be ugly and brutal
- Superman rejects OZ's plan
- Oz: "I didn't want to have to do this, but if you're not going to leave willingly I'll MAKE you leave"
- Part four:
- Conflict over plan, Superman v. OZ
- OZ unleashes his full power
- "I'll show you how easy it is to corrupt humans" — his agents have been set up to bring about the end of the world
- Superman succeeds in freeing OZ's agents and thwarting the plan, but humanity continues destroying itself on its own
- Jon sides with OZ (or seems to)
- Part Five: similar pacing/beats to detective story
- Superman v. OZ
- Earth is saved, OZ is defeated
- OZ is plucked away by a bright blue light, the experiment completed and sent to parts unknown.
- Superman believes mr. oz to be dead, takes his staff and places it in the fortress
- Superman is now doubtful in humanity, hearing negativity to echo pt1's opening – also echoes detective ending